DOLLHOUSE
CONSTRUCTION and RESTORATION

DOLLHOUSE
CONSTRUCTION and RESTORATION

Nina Glenn Joyner

Chilton Book Company

Radnor, Pennsylvania

Copyright © 1977 by Nina Glenn Joyner
All Rights Reserved
Published in Radnor, Pennsylvania, by Chilton Book Company
and simultaneously in Don Mills, Ontario, Canada,
by Thomas Nelson & Sons, Ltd.
Manufactured in the United States of America

Library of Congress Cataloging in Publication Data
Joyner, Nina Glenn.
   Dollhouse construction and restoration.

   (Chilton's creative crafts series)
   Includes index.
   1. Doll-houses. I. Title.
TT175.3.J68   1977   745.59′23   77-6117
ISBN 0-8019-6462-8
ISBN 0-8019-6463-6 pbk.

2 3 4 5 6 7 8 9 0   6 5 4 3 2 1 0 9 8

To
COURTNEY, CLAUDE, *and* GLENN

Contents

Acknowledgments

This book could never have been completed without the help of many people. The artists were Howard Shockey, who furnished all but three of the line drawings (as well as some mathematical calculations and a bit of good humor); Charles Crouch, who contributed the balance of the line drawings; Margaret Dornin, another superb artist, who was the landscape designer; Edward Wanchok, who helped design the houses; Leonard Wanchok, who drew the plans; and Francesco Mauro, the artist with the saw.

Most of the photographs were taken by Thomas Snell and Kenneth Balzar. A few were contributed by Brian Simmons. Last but not least to thank are Courtney Joyner and Joe Montello, who always seem to end up doing the leg work. There is no way to properly thank all the friends who donated their time and their dollhouses.

DOLLHOUSE
CONSTRUCTION and RESTORATION

Introduction

Every person in the world has a dream and for some people this dream is a house. This need not be "an impossible dream" since, for everyone who desires it, this dream can be fulfilled in miniature. As in real life, the person who does not want to build can find an old house and restore it.

No matter what the limitations of your real-life dwelling, only a relatively small expenditure in money is needed to build or restore the dollhouse of your dreams. If you were building a dream house for real, you might be easily deterred by unions and strikes. With the dollhouse which you will construct, there will be no such problems involved. You are the plumber, the contractor, the electrician, and the decorator. This is your dream and no one else can interfere.

Although many dollhouses house dolls, most of them are built for people. A "person-size" house with its furnishings, landscaping, and accessories might be lacking completely in both charm and personality, whereas its doll-size counterpart would be enchanting.

This book is for people who think dollhouses really are for people, and who would like to build one from scratch or restore an old one which was a lucky find in an antique store.

In spite of the fact that construction of a dollhouse hardly falls into the category of building a real house, there is still a certain amount of planning necessary before the actual building begins. What kind of dollhouse do you want? Is this house to be for your children or grandchildren to enjoy, or is it being built for you, as an adult, to finish in great detail to house your miniature treasures?

Where does one keep a dollhouse? Obviously, if it is built as a present for a child, the house certainly should be in the child's bedroom or playroom. However, if it is being constructed as an adult treasure house, it should be proudly displayed in the living room or den, if possible. Hopefully, it will be displayed as the center of attention and will be seen from all sides. If it must be against a wall, with only the back showing, then practically no detail work would be necessary for the front of the house.

A major point to consider is the size of the house. As when building a real house, only you know what size is most suitable for your particular circumstances. There is one tremendous advantage that building a dollhouse has over building a real house: all the houses in this book were built for $30 or less. The cost of $30 assumes that all the materials for the house will have to be bought and, of course, many people have small scraps of wood and other materials around which can be used.

There are plans in this book for six architectural styles: log cabin, contemporary, Spanish, southern plantation house, Victorian, and New England saltbox.

The only design that does not give the builder much leeway for flights of fancy in the exterior trim is the log cabin for, as everyone knows, a log cabin is a log cabin is a log cabin.

CHAPTER 1 *How to Begin*

A dollhouse must be well planned and well thought out before the actual construction starts, so the only place to begin is on paper. First, decide how much money you can afford to spend. As mentioned in the Introduction, a very good and sturdy dollhouse can be built for about $30. Naturally, one can spend a great deal more on interior decorating, but to have a good, well-built, and attractive house, one does not need an unlimited bank account.

If there is a normal amount of space available to place the dollhouse after construction is complete, then the best scale to use is one inch to one foot (1:12). This is a standard scale for dollhouses; practically all furnishings and accessories manufactured today are made to this scale. You will find that many of the old or antique dollhouses are not built to any particular scale at all and are exact replicas of houses that existed at the time.

Will you have a one or two-story house? Whichever the choice, the details are minor. There is simply a change in roof design. In the one-story contemporary house, the roof is designed to be removed entirely. When building a dollhouse, there is always one thing to remember, no matter how many stories tall it is. You want the rooms to be reachable while working on it and both the rooms and furnishings to be visible when completed. It is for this reason that many of the rooms in the dollhouses in this book are separated by room dividers rather than by solid walls with doors, although there are two that are designed with some solid walls for more realism.

SELECTING AN ARCHITECTURAL STYLE

Before you start to build, you have to know the type of dollhouse you want. Decide first how much money is to be spent and study the various types of houses and plans in this book. With the exception of the log cabin, all the houses can be much more elaborate than pictured, since none of these costs more than $30.

The log cabin and the New England saltbox are both 30 inches wide. The size and design of the cabin is based on real ones scattered throughout western

3

Pennsylvania—they were given in lieu of money to soldiers who fought in the American Revolution.

The other houses in this book have frontages which range from 32 to 36 inches. If measured in feet, each size would be appropriate for each style of house.

If one plans to add landscaping, then another 6 to 8 inches are added to the front and two sides as a base. This, of course, requires more space—possibly more than is available. It is very easy to cut down the size of any of these houses without changing the relative scale. The scale is very important, since nearly all furnishings which one might want to buy are scaled 1:12.

SUPPLIES

After you have decided upon the style of the house, the next step is to buy graph paper. Then study the architectural plans for the dream house of your choice and, on the graph paper, make any necessary changes in size. The house may even be drawn full size on poster board. This might be easier to follow.

Once the decision on style and size has been made, do not rush out to buy all the materials that you think might be needed. Naturally, there are basic materials around the house or apartment you'll find once your thoughts are steered in the direction of constructing a dollhouse. There are certain basic materials which you will need for any of the dollhouses, with the exception of the log cabin. That is a much more simple house and does not require moldings or interior finishing.

The materials list for each project includes itemized prices reflecting exactly what it cost the author to build the house. This will fluctuate with rising prices and additions or omissions made by you to the basic house plans. Specific amounts will also vary with geographical location.

Basic Construction Materials

The sturdiest building material is ³/₈-inch plywood. You can use ¹/₄-inch plywood, as well as ¹/₄-inch Masonite. Always remember to buy second grade when purchasing the plywood, if possible. Seconds save quite a bit of money. There is little difference between the cost of Masonite and plywood seconds. In 1976, the cost of ¹/₄-inch Masonite was $3.95 for a 4 by 8-foot section; ¹/₄-inch plywood seconds cost $4, so the plywood would certainly be the first choice. However, seconds are not always easy to find. The ³/₈-inch plywood is considerably more expensive; a 4 by 8-foot piece of this thickness can cost between $7 and $10.

One good way to save money on construction is to buy scraps of wood, since the largest piece of wood needed for any of the dollhouses in this book is

36 by 36 inches. All lumberyards have scraps and sell them very cheaply. The point is to keep your basic construction costs as low as possible. As you progress with your building, you will find that the cost of paint, brushes, stains, windows, and moldings can add up very quickly.

Interior Moldings

For interior moldings, balsa wood is ideal. It is light and easy to glue and takes paint or stain very well. All craft and hobby stores carry balsa wood strips. A 3/8-inch-square strip of balsa, about 20 inches long, costs about 15¢. A dozen of these can be used easily in the average house. As always, interior moldings made especially for dollhouses can be bought, but these are expensive and not for the person with an eye on his wallet.

Roofing Materials

Roofing materials can be as simple or as complicated as you wish. The easiest and cheapest way to make not only a perfectly acceptable, but very good-looking, roof is to paint it a color that goes well with the house. Then, when the paint is dry, use a felt-tip marking pen to draw shingles. Real shingles can be made from the thinnest balsa wood and attached with glue to the unpainted roof. Roofing material made for dollhouses may be bought but, once again, this runs into money.

Windows

There are several choices for windows. One is almost as effective as the next, insofar as appearance is concerned. It again depends on the amount of money one wishes to spend. There are thin glass, such as picture frame glass; Plexiglas; heavy plastic, such as the type used for picture holders in wallets or for term-paper binders. Sheet plastic can be bought in hobby shops: This is a very good, very clear plastic and costs about 75¢ for a 2 by 3-foot piece. Plastic is used almost entirely in commercially built dollhouses—even the ones costing more than $100.

Windows made just for dollhouses may be bought; these are expensive and often will not fit the openings of a noncommercial dollhouse. In some cases, it will take one and a half or two dollhouse windows to fit a noncommercial house. Ten of these windows in a package can cost as much as $2.50.

The homemade plastic windows can be very attractive if, instead of painting the stripping to make panes, one uses thin strips of balsa wood which have been painted and glued onto the window. The thin glass is *not* recommended if the house is to be used by a child. The danger of breakage is too great. This glass, too, can become expensive if one has to pay to have it cut.

The best window material for a professional finished appearance is Plexiglas. This is extremely expensive and can cost as much as $15 or $20 if it is cut to size. Plexiglas *can* be bought by the sheet and cut at home if there is a power saw available. Goggles must be worn when doing the cutting because Plexiglas tends to splinter.

If a stained-glass window is wanted, as shown above the door in the Victorian house, greeting cards are a great source of supply. Many cards have plastic stained-glass windows attached to them and these work beautifully.

Hardware

Very little of the hardware used in building a dollhouse will have to be bought. Hinges for the doors are about the only type of hardware that it will be necessary to buy. Everything else, such as curtain rods, towel racks, doorknobs, and door knockers, will be made from anything from small plastic straws to a broken earring. All the aforementioned hardware *can* be bought and is perfectly to scale, but doing it yourself is not just a matter of saving money: it is the fun of using your imagination and seeing a fine brass door knocker where someone else would see only the back of a clip-on earring.

TOOLS

The only tools required for building a dollhouse, aside from the ordinary household hammers, pliers, and screwdrivers, are an electric drill and an electric hand jigsaw. Both the drill and the jigsaw can be rented, but power tools have come down in price in recent years; since use of these tools would not be limited to the building of one dollhouse, the purchase of these would be a good investment.

Renting power tools is a good idea if, for example, a saw is rented on Friday and the cutting job completed by Sunday evening. Many rental agencies will not charge for Sunday use, since they are closed. However, if the building and construction is going to occur just in the evenings for an hour or two, it would be worth your while to buy rather than rent the power tools. Hardware stores have specials on these from time to time, and they can be bought for as little as $7 or $8.

LIGHTS AND ELECTRIC POWER

To be especially effective, a dollhouse needs electric lights—not people-sized lights, and not even Christmas tree lights, although these can be used in a certain way if other lighting is not feasible. The lighting system, although it will be almost the final step in building the house, should be planned from the beginning.

Supplies

The power for electricity can come from one of two sources if commercial scale-size dollhouse wire and lighting fixtures are used. One source is a lantern or six-volt battery. The other source is a small transformer designed for this purpose. These transformers range in power to accommodate from three to twenty-two light bulbs in a dollhouse.

If a six-volt battery is used for power, then foreign-made bulbs should also be used. Available in hobby and dollhouse supply stores, foreign-made bulbs are of smaller voltage than the American ones. With either type of power there are two things to be considered: how to house the battery or transformer and where to drill holes in the walls or ceilings so that the wiring will be unobtrusive.

Wiring for electricity will not be shown on the architectural plans for the dollhouses, since the builder will have to determine the type, amount, and location of fixtures and wiring. The idea now is to keep in mind the type of wiring while building and to know where lights will be placed in the completed house. If battery-powered lights are used, then the builder might want to add a shed, garage, or some type of outbuilding to house the battery, so that it will not be an eyesore when the dream house is finished.

There are many miniature lamps available today that have their own tiny built-in batteries. If you use these, wiring the house is not necessary. However, these lamps are expensive and you might not want to invest in enough for an entire house, since they cost about $6 apiece.

Installing Electrical Wiring

There is something very special about a dollhouse with electric lights and wiring a house does not have to be either difficult or expensive. If the decision to wire a house is made before building, holes are drilled in the ceilings before assembling the house. If you are restoring one or decide to wire after the building is complete, the walls can be grooved just deep enough for the wire to be set in the wood, then covered with wallpaper. Or, in the case of a painted wall, a strip of molding can be added. There is no need for the wires to show. If the wires are run along the floor, they can be covered with a rug.

First, decide how many lights will be needed and buy a transformer of the proper size. Figure 1-1 shows a transformer for three lights and one for twenty-two lights. The three-light version was $5 and the larger version $9.50. Before actually buying the transformer, whatever the size, test it for voltage before taking it home. Some will be marked with a certain voltage but, when tested, not have that much power. Detailed instructions for wiring come with most transformers.

For parallel wiring, Fig. 1-2 shows the basic principles. The transformer has two terminals and a strip of 22-gauge copper wire (covered, of course) is at-

Fig. 1–1 *At left*, transformer for twenty-two lights; *right*, transformer for three dollhouse lights

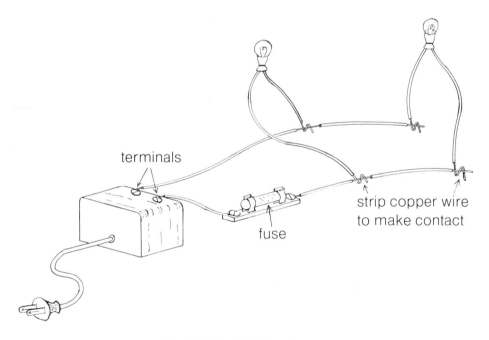

Fig. 1–2   Parallel wiring diagram

tached to each terminal. One piece of wire has the fuse set in. Each light has two wires. Trim the rubber or plastic coating a little bit on the main wires so that enough copper is exposed to make contact and attach one of the light wires to one side and one to the other. Continue with this until all the lights that are needed have been connected.

The type of transformer shown in Fig. 1-1 is not recommended, since it does not have a plug that will fit an extension cord. If this kind is used, buy an extension cord with a female plug; remove the plug and connect to the small transformer with tape. Be careful that no wires are plugged into electrical power while working.

There are many sources for buying dollhouse lighting, but a less expensive way is to buy lights for train sets—the type used inside a building. These are good for ceiling lights and covers can be made for them. Instead of paying several dollars for a light, the cost will be only 25¢ or 50¢.

Do not do your wiring in series—when one light goes out, they all go out. Parallel wiring is easier to do.

ASSEMBLING THE DOLLHOUSES

With the exceptions of the log cabin and the contemporary house, the assembly of all other houses is basically the same.

Preparing the Parts

Do as much of the interior decorating and carpentry as possible before putting the house together. This includes installation of windows and doors, papering, painting, and staining of walls, floors, and ceilings. First-floor ceilings are especially hard to reach once the house has been assembled.

If 3/16-inch plywood is used for the construction of the house, then support other than the dividing walls will be needed to keep the house sturdy. One-inch triangular molding is perfect for this (Fig. 1-3).

If 3/8-inch plywood is used to build the house, then there is no need for support other than the interior walls of the first floor—and second floor, if there is a third floor.

Raising the Walls

The basic assembly of any two-story house is very simple.

Step 1. Take the three exterior walls (front and two sides), which are completely finished, with windows and doors in place and interior papering and painting complete. You will note on each cutting diagram that the front piece is cut the full width of the house. Side walls are butted inside the front edge and nails hammered through the front piece and into the side wall plywood. Use small finishing nails so the wood will not split.

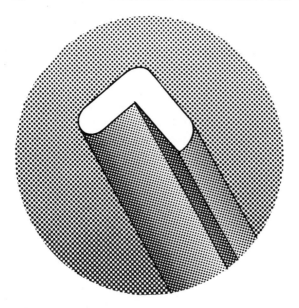

Fig. 1–3   One-inch triangular molding for supports

Fig. 1–4   Three sides of the house are nailed to the base

Step 2. Take the base or first floor, which has been cut to proper size and stained or finished, and place the open walls which are nailed together in position on the base. The exterior shell can be glued in place with Contact cement if all pieces form a perfectly level, even seam. For a sturdier house, however, it is best to nail them in place, through the base from underneath and into the exterior wall plywood. At this point, you have a three-sided box (Fig. 1-4).

Step 3. Following the appropriate floor plan, nail the dividing walls of the first floor to the ceiling of the first floor which, of course, is also the second-story *floor* (Fig. 1-5).

Step 4. Next, install the dividing walls and first-story ceiling (or second-story floor) inside the house by nailing this unit to the three outside walls. One of the reasons for the molding on the Spanish house is to hide the nailheads on the stucco. On the other houses, these can simply be painted over.

Step 5. The interior second-floor dividing walls are now installed and nailed to the front and sides of the house. Attach the roof, following the specific instructions for the architectural style you are building.

Step 6. Paint the exterior. Cut and paint the shutters and attach them with epoxy or Elmer's glue. While drying, the shutters may be held in place with straight pins.

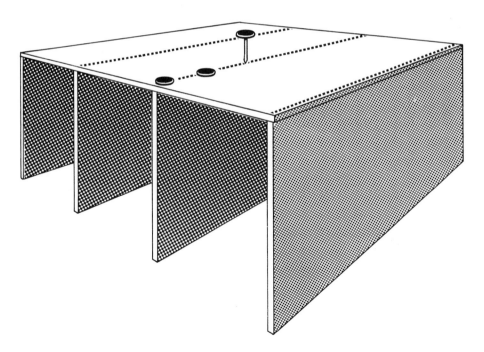

Fig. 1–5   The first-floor interior walls are nailed to the second-story floor

CHAPTER 2 *Authentic Log Cabin*

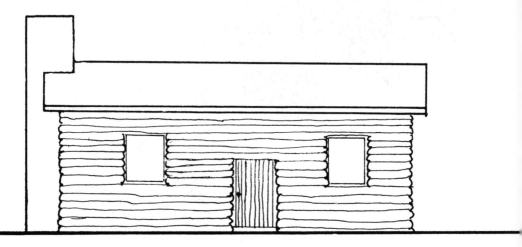

Fig. 2–1   Architect's drawing of log cabin

DOWEL LENGTHS REQUIRED

You will need 20 dowels, ⁵/₈-inch diameter. All are 36 inches long and cost will vary from 32¢ to 50¢ apiece, so it is worthwhile to price them at several places.

Four 30″ dowels	Three 7¹/₂″ dowels
Twenty 17″ dowels	Three 7¹/₄″ dowels
Six 14³/₄″ dowels	Sixteen 6″ dowels
Three 13¹/₄″ dowels	Three 5³/₄″ dowels
Six 11³/₄″ dowels	Nine 4¹/₄″ dowels
Three 7³/₄″ dowels	Six 2¹/₂″ dowels

MATERIALS REQUIRED

³/₈″ plywood—4′ × 8′ (a 2′ × 4′ piece will be used for the base)	$ 4.00
Two tubes of white interior *latex* caulk and caulking gun (gun optional)	3.00
Dowels (as above)	6.50
One 2′ to 3′ = square scrap of ¹/₄″ Masonite	2.00
Three strips of balsa wood, 36″ long, ¹/₂″ deep, and ¹/₄″ wide (these will be your beams and fireplace mantel)	.50
Plexiglas windows cut to order—three 2″ × 2″ windows and two 3¹/₂″ × 5″ windows (plastic will not be nearly as effective for these, as the Plexiglas can be set *in* the window opening	4.00
The loft (if desired) will be of ³/₈″ plywood, 17¹/₂″ wide by 8¹/₂″ long	.50
Five-pound bag of Sacrete mortar mix	1.00
Scraps of balsa wood or any other thin wood, such as a cigar box, to make the base for the chimney and fireplace (do not use heavy cardboard for this, as the water from the cement will cause it to collapse)	.25
Half-pint can of wood stain	.50
Cellophane tape	.50
Yardstick, ruler, or tape measure—a 6″ ruler or a metal tape measure is better than a yardstick once the actual building starts, because a yardstick gets in the way	—
Glue—Elmer's, Goodyear Pliobond, or model airplane glue	1.00
An old table knife for spreading the latex and the masonry	—
A scrap of leather from an old belt	—
	$23.75

With minor exceptions, the log cabin shown here is an authentic replica of the type given to soldiers by General Anthony Wayne after the American Revolution. These cabins are scattered throughout western Pennsylvania and were given to the soldiers in lieu of money, since cash was in short supply. The principal deviation from authenticity in building the cabin, shown in Figs. 2-1, 2-2, and color Fig. 1, is that the logs are not notched. If the cabin is being built for a child to enjoy, she certainly will not mind such an omission, since it would be extremely time consuming for the builder. As it is, the cabin easily can be built in three or four evenings or over a weekend.

If you enjoy building this log cabin, it is a relatively simple matter to design your own variation. Make a full-size floor plan for the dollhouse you want to build, incorporating the structural changes and altering the positions of doors and windows to correspond to the real-life version of the cabin you are copying. Log cabin styles varied greatly in details, depending on climate and materials available as the frontier moved West.

SUPPLIES AND PREPARATION

With the exception of the plywood and the Masonite, all materials can be bought at a hardware store or hobby shop. The total cost for materials was $23.63. This included $4 for professionally cut Plexiglas windows. If plastic is used for the windows, that cost would be only about 50¢.

As with any other project, several preliminary steps have to be taken before the actual fun of building can begin. The first step is to find a place to work. You do not need a special work room for this project; the cabin was built on a card table. After the decision has been made about where to work, then the materials must be prepared.

The second step is to stain the dowels; since they come in 36-inch lengths, it is much faster to stain them all at once, then cut them into the required lengths. After the "logs" are in place, the cut ends can be stained all at the same time. The accompanying materials list shows the number of dowels of each size required: all are ⅝-inch diameter (Fig. 2-3). Measure very carefully. It is a

14

Fig. 2–2   Authentic log cabin replica

nuisance to mismeasure, miscut, then have to make another trip to the hardware store for more dowels that then have to be stained, measured, and cut. Faulty measuring also will add to the cost of the dollhouse. When measuring, since there are so many lengths required, try to get the most out of one 36-inch dowel, wasting as little as possible.

When cutting the logs, the power jigsaw will be your most valuable tool. The wood from which dowels are made is extremely hard. Cutting that would

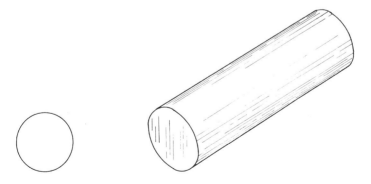

Fig. 2–3   Drawing of $\frac{5}{8}''$ dowel, actual size

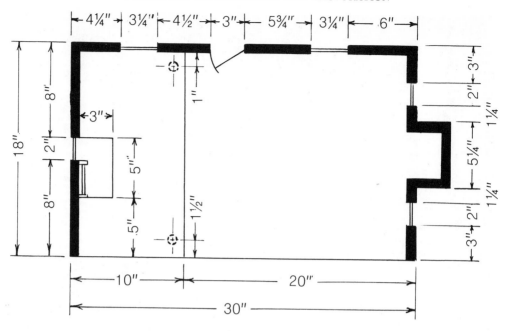

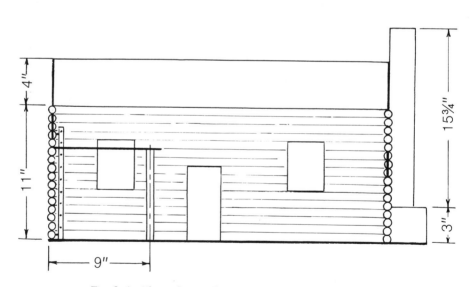

Fig. 2–4   Floor plans and exterior measurements for cabin

take several minutes for each by hand can be accomplished in seconds on the power saw.

The actual size of the cabin is 30 inches long, 18 inches deep, and 15¼ inches high, not including the chimney which, of course, extends 3 inches beyond the house and 4 inches above (Fig. 2-4). Because of the chimney, it is better to have a plywood base. Since it is built of masonry, if there is not a good sturdy base, the weight of the chimney might cause it to become detached. In every case except the base, Masonite may be substituted for plywood listed in the materials section.

In the construction of the log cabin, the best way to begin is to stain all the wood that you will be using. This includes not only the dowels, but the roof, the loft (if there is one), and the balsa strips for the beams and fireplace mantel. The stain dries very quickly: By the time the last pieces of wood have been stained, the first pieces will be ready to measure and cut. A black felt-tip pen is an excellent marker for this, as it will be difficult to see pencil marks through the stain.

CONSTRUCTING EXTERIOR WALLS

After all the dowels have been cut, next cut out the base and place it on a card table, where the work of building will proceed. Study Figs. 2-5 and 2-6,

Fig. 2–5 Placement of logs as three sides are built up simultaneously

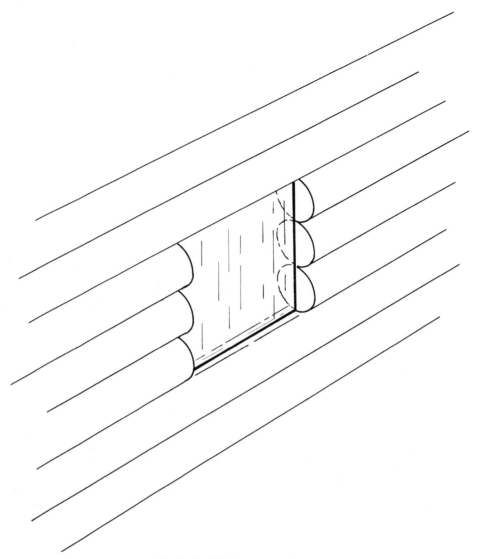

Fig. 2–6   Window set into logs

showing the placement of the proper-sized logs both on the front and at each end of the cabin. The entire cabin is built simultaneously, rather than doing one section at a time. The reason for this is to give the latex "mortar" time to set. If more than two or three logs are stacked before the mortar has a chance to dry completely, the wall will collapse.

The first logs on all three sides—the base logs—are attached to the base with a strong glue, such as Weldwood, Elmer's, or Pliobond. When the base logs have dried (which does not take very long), then add the mortar and the next log, and continue in this manner. When applying the mortar, be sure that you do not use too much. Apply it as if you were putting toothpaste on a toothbrush—that is about how it will look. Next place another log on top of the mortar, then take a table knife and flatten the mortar between the logs, both inside and out. Without flattening and smoothing the caulk, it would end up looking more like cake icing than mortar.

As log on top of log is added, remember the measurements for doors, windows, and fireplace. The fireplace can always be adjusted to fit whatever space is left between the walls at the end of the cabin, but if precut Plexiglas windows are used, they must fit exactly *in* the windows, not against the logs (Fig. 2-6).

ADDING WINDOWS, DOOR, AND LOFT

Putting this log cabin together is about the same as doing a giant jigsaw puzzle. When the three walls are sixteen logs high, it is time to stop building and take a look at interior details which will follow before the ceiling is put on top or the loft is installed.

This is when the windows and door are put in place. If there are any scraps of old wood available, a rough door with a hand-hewn look is most effective. The door handle and hinges are made from leather strips slightly more than an inch long and ¼ inch wide. Notice that the door handle is wider at each end (Fig. 2-7). The leather "hardware" is applied with glue. The hinges

Fig. 2–7 Rough-hewn cabin
door with leather handle

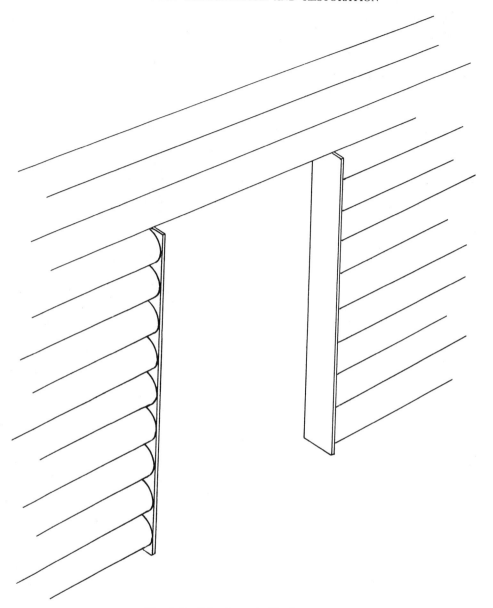

Fig. 2–8   Balsa frame inside doorway

are attached to the balsa frame inside the doorway (Fig. 2-8). When the glue has dried on the frame, the door may be hung.

If a loft is desired, this may be put in now. As you can see in Fig. 2-9, there is no loft in this particular cabin. However, one can be installed easily and makes the cabin authentic in design. The dimensions

Fig. 2–9   Interior of the log cabin

of the loft should be approximately 8 by 17 inches, depending on the placement of the log walls. It is 7 inches above the floor, or one log below the single small window (Fig. 2-10). A square of 2½ by 4 inches is cut on the window side of the loft. The loft can be glued to the logs with contact cement and supported by two dowels, slightly less than 7 inches high, to allow for the thickness of the plywood or Masonite. A ladder of balsa can be built and propped against the cutout for access to the loft.

RAISING THE ROOF

The ceiling is put on next and requires nothing more than contact cement to hold it in place and just one small nail at each corner. You will be happy to discover that your cabin is sturdy enough to withstand the pounding of a hammer. The ceiling serves two purposes—one is as a ceiling for the first floor, to which beams can be attached, and the other is as a base for the roof supports. As you can see in Fig. 2-11, these supports are nothing more than two triangles, 18 inches long and 4 inches high at the apex. The roof supports are attached with glue to the ceiling and, once again, a small nail at each end is used to steady the support.

The next step is to put on the roof, which is in two sections. The front half of the roof is 11¾ inches wide and 30 inches long. This allows for a 1½-inch overhang across the front of the cabin. The front roof is attached with small nails.

The back roof is 9⅝ inches wide, 30 inches long and is attached only with leather hinges to the front part, so that it can be lifted to show the storage area.

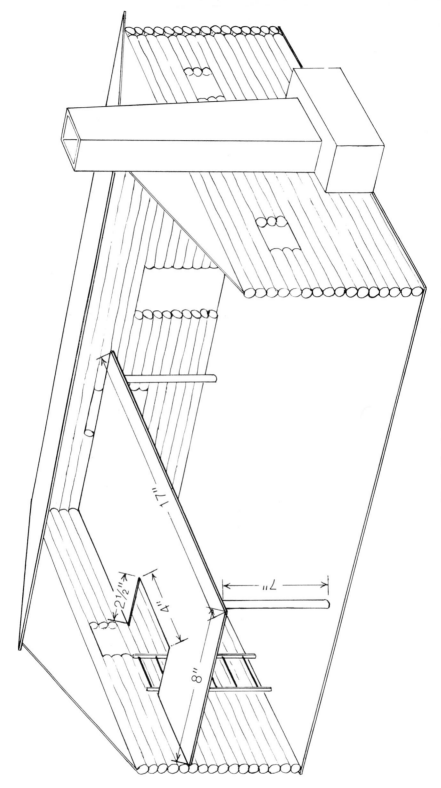

Fig. 2-10 Loft dimensions and placement

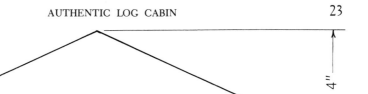

Fig. 2–11   Triangular roof supports

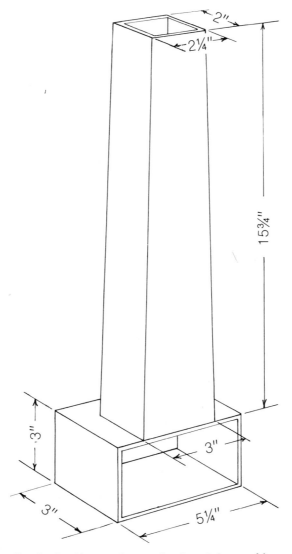

Fig. 2–12   Chimney base made of two balsa wood boxes

BUILDING THE CHIMNEY AND FIREPLACE

Once the roof is on the cabin, the time has come to start building the fireplace and chimney. This is probably the most fun of the entire project, since not many dollhouses have *real* chimneys.

To begin, one must first build two boxes of balsa or any other light wood. Balsa was used in this case, since it can be cut with a razor, and no more sawing is necessary. The chimney base is made from a box $5^1/_4$ inches wide, 3 inches high, and 3 inches deep (Fig. 2-12). The second part of the chimney is a box that starts out 3 inches wide and diminishes to $2^1/_4$ inches wide at the top and 2 inches deep: This part of the chimney is $15^3/_4$ inches high (Fig. 2-12).

After the frames for the chimney have been built, they are attached to the cabin with real mortar. Mix Sacrete in a plastic quart container with enough water to make the mortar easy to handle but not runny. This can be applied either with an old table knife or tongue depressors. The mortar should be built up very gradually; otherwise, it will be too heavy and fall off the balsa wood base. Of course, the fireplace is built at this time. Coat the inside of the balsa box with mortar and bring it out around the logs to build a hearth, just as if this were a real fireplace (Fig. 2-13). After a day or two, as the mortar dries, the chimney will become slightly detached from the cabin. Mix up a little more

Fig. 2–13   Fireplace and mantel in cabin interior

mortar and fill in the cracks. This slight separation will occur over a period of a week or more—maybe even a few weeks—just as a new house settles. Simply add more mortar. It does not take much at a time—half a cup at the most.

The final step in finishing the log cabin is to add the mantel and the beams. The mantel will be 6½ inches long and ½ inch wide. For the beams, you will need four strips of balsa 17½ inches long, ½ inch deep, and ¼ inch wide. Space them equally across the ceiling as shown in Fig. 2-9 and attach with glue. The log cabin is complete and ready to furnish.

If there are older children in the family, boys as well as girls enjoy building the log cabin and claim that it is more fun than model airplanes.

CHAPTER 3 *Contemporary Dollhouse*

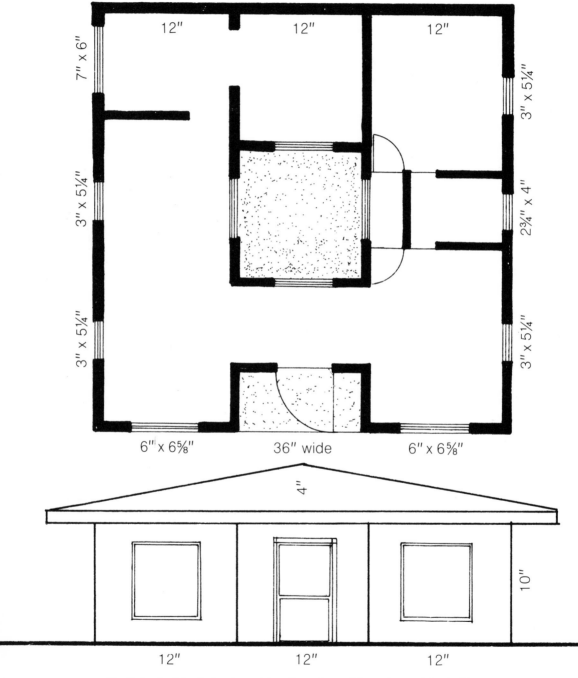

Fig. 3–1   Architect's drawing, giving dimensions of floor plan and front of house

MATERIALS REQUIRED

One piece of 4' × 8' plywood	$4.00
One piece of 4' × 4' plywood	2.00
One piece of 3' × 4' Masonite	3.00
Three pieces of 6" × 10" Plexiglas	6.00
Heavy plastic for the windows (two 2' × 3' sheets)	.50
Half-pint can of wood stain	.50
Mirror for atrium pond	.25
Half pint of enamel for exterior main color	.50
Half pint of enamel for roof	.50
Half pint of enamel for constrasting strips on exterior	.50
Weldwood or Pliobond glue	1.00
Very small finishing nails	.50
Fourteen strips of balsa, 36" long and $1/8$" × $1/8$" thick (342")	2.00
Three 1" hinges for roof	.75
One pair $1/2$" hinges for front door	.75
Two 36" strips of $3/4$" molding to go across front and back of house at roof line	1.50
	$24.25

This contemporary dollhouse has two unusual features not often found in regular dollhouses. There is an atrium with a pond and an art gallery. The house is large by dollhouse standards. The ceilings are high and the rooms are oversized. The reason for this is that it is a one-story house (Figs. 3-1, 3-2, and color Fig. 2). However, the size easily can be adjusted to fit whatever space is available. Be sure always, though, to keep the 1:12 scale.

SUPPLIES AND PREPARATION

The contemporary design is relatively inexpensive to build—even using $6 worth of Plexiglas for the atrium. This house was built from 3/16-inch plywood, except for the Masonite roof. One piece of 4 by 8-foot plywood, one piece of 4 by 4-foot plywood, and one piece of 3 by 4-foot Masonite will be ample for the construction. With the exception of a plywood base 3 feet square, the entire house can be built of Masonite. Plywood *is* better for the interior hall walls,

Fig. 3–2 Contemporary house—atrium has pond and art gallery

28

since it can be stained. The floors also are stained. The vertical stripping on the exterior is of balsa wood.

All wall and floor coverings are cut from scraps of cloth and gift-wrap paper. The burlap used on the wall of the front hall was bought in a craft shop and was prepasted.

This dollhouse is one where the builder will find the use of a power jigsaw essential. If it is more convenient to rent rather than to buy one, all the cutting can be done in an evening if you get an early start.

This is a "pre-fab" house and wood cutting is the only real labor involved. If it is not going to be put together within a matter of a few days, it is extremely important to mark each piece of wood as it is cut. Be sure to mark on the *inside* wall and not the outside, since the labeling will not always come off and, on an inside wall, can be covered with paper.

MEASURING AND CUTTING

When cutting plywood, be sure that the blade of the saw is not too coarse. A blade which is too coarse will cause splitting; later, the wood will have to be sanded or even filled in with wood filler. Fig. 3-1 supplies a floor plan with all parts in position; Fig. 3-4 is a layout for cutting.

Front of house is one piece of 36 by 14-inch plywood or Masonite. The porch is cut from the center, 12 inches wide and 10 inches high. The peak of the roof is 14 inches high. There is a picture window on either side of the porch: Each window is 6 by 6⅝ inches. The opening for each window should be 2 inches from the top, 2 inches from the bottom, and 2⅝ inches from each side, as shown in Fig. 3-3.

The Porch is made from four 4 by 10-inch strips.

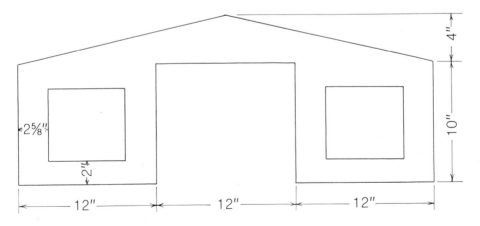

Fig. 3–3 Dimensions for front of house

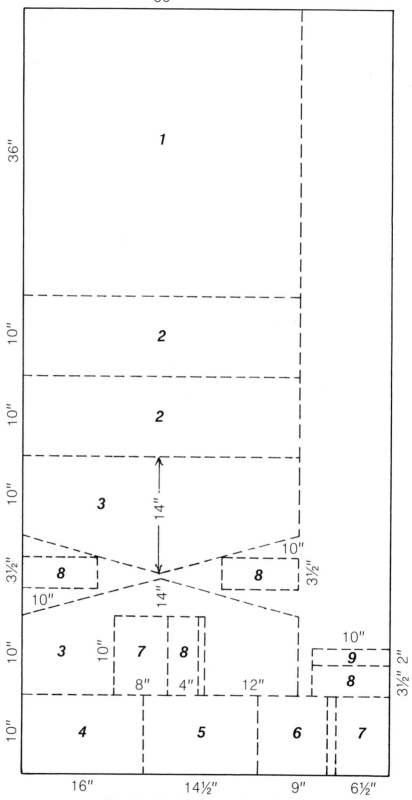

Fig. 3–4 Cutting diagram for wood pieces

Back of house is cut exactly the same as the front, but there is only one picture window.

Right or bedroom side is cut 10 by 36 inches, with three windows. The end windows will be 2½ inches from the bottom of the house and 6 inches from each end. These windows are 5¼ inches high and 3 inches wide. The middle or bathroom window is higher and smaller than the other two, since most real bathroom windows are that way. This window is 4 inches from the base, 2¾ inches wide and 4 inches high. This is centered between the other two and is approximately 7½ inches from each of the other windows.

Lefthand or living room and kitchen side has three windows, two small and one large. The large window is on the kitchen wall and is 7 by 6 inches and 2½ inches from the base of the house. There is about 6 inches to the middle window. The middle window is 3½ inches from the base and measures 3 by 5¼ inches and is 7 inches from the next window, which is the one nearest the front of the house. The front window is the same, 3 by 5¼ inches, and 3½ inches from the base.

The inside walls are much easier to cut, since there are no windows:

Divider between living room and kitchen, 9″ × 10″
Back hall and bedroom wall, 10″ × 14½″
Front hall and front bedroom wall, 10″ × 16″
Entrance hall dividers, 2¼″ × 10″, placed 7½″ from the front entrance
Bathroom walls are both 7″ × 10″—placed 14½″ down the front bedroom
    wall and 15″ down the back bedroom wall (the bathroom is 6″ wide)
Divider between bathroom and hall, 4″ × 10″

The two strips of molding for both the front and back of the house, each 36 inches long, will complete the cutting. Precise figures are a bore, and it is not necessary at all to use these exact figures. This house is supposed to be the way you want it, and if you want the windows larger or smaller, that is what makes building a dollhouse fun. Move the walls around. Make the bedrooms smaller and the bathroom larger. Add a dining room. This is a flexible plan. It is easily changed.

ASSEMBLING THE WALLS

When the cutting is complete, the house can be put together entirely with glue. Weldwood or Pliobond will do a good job. This is when the cellophane tape will be handy. As angles are pressed together, the tape does a good job of holding until the glue is dry. Small nails can be used for extra strength if desired. Follow the general directions in Chapter 1 for assembling walls.

Before placing the house on the base, it is a good idea to stain the floor. Then, after the house has been divided into rooms, one may finish the floors with carpeting or linoleum or leave them natural. Also, if you know, for instance, that the living room is going to be white, paint these walls before gluing them together. Thus, the danger of getting paint on the floor is eliminated, and it is far easier to paint on a flat surface than inside after the walls are in place.

FINISHING WALLS AND WINDOWS

Decorating the interior is more exciting than doing the inside of a real house. There is no need to worry about the price per roll of wallpaper. Even before the building starts, you will be thinking about the interior and, everytime you go in a dime store or gift shop, you will find yourself looking at wrapping paper for the walls and notepaper or greeting cards for "murals" and "paintings." There is one material that seems to be a natural for kitchen or bathroom floors, and that's Contact. However, except for the solid colors, all the patterns are too large, even the wood-grained ones. Since the special paper made just for dollhouses is fairly expensive, and since other papers and fabrics with tiny patterns are so cheap and readily available, it is not necessary to spend a lot of money. Do keep one thing in mind, though: If the paper chosen has a floral pattern of, perhaps, 1/2 inch, think whether you would like flowers 6 inches across on your own walls. Remember your 1:12 scale.

Elmer's glue is fine for use as wallpaper paste with fabric as well as paper. Because the contemporary dollhouse does not have ceilings, all wallpaper should be trimmed as neatly as possible so that it looks as nice looking "down" as looking "in."

When the interior walls are finished, install the windows. If Plexiglas is used for a window on any wall that has been papered, Elmer's glue can be used to affix it. On any painted wall, Weldwood or Pliobond is necessary. Since neither of these bonds dry clear, some kind of molding should be put around the windows to hide the glue. The moldings can be of thin blasa which has been painted or decorated with fabric braid to blend or contrast with the painted wall. Small plastic drinking straws about 1/16 inch in diameter make perfect curtain

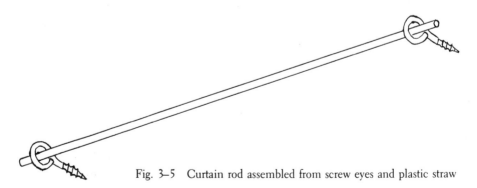

Fig. 3–5   Curtain rod assembled from screw eyes and plastic straw

rods. Use very small eye screws for the hangers (Fig. 3-5). Before putting up the curtain rods, they may be painted either silver or gold.

INSTALLING THE ATRIUM

The atrium is built from three pieces of 6 by 10-inch Plexiglas as shown in Fig. 3-6., This is not glued to the floor, since the owner of this dollhouse might want to change things around once in a while. The pond in the atrium is a dime-store purse mirror. Finding such a simple mirror is not easy. Craft shops that carry materials for decoupage do have mirrors without frames. If one without a frame cannot be found, just cover the edges of the mirror with glue and coat with light sand. Put whatever small plants you like in the atrium, or even make a vine to climb up the sides. Small dabs of florist's clay will hold artificial plants or live air plants in place (see Fig. 8-2).

The paintings in the art gallery are from greeting cards and old art books bought at flea markets and school fairs. The frames are of braid or ribbon. The paintings are not glued to the walls. They are attached with floral clay, which makes for easy removal if one decides to change them from time to time.

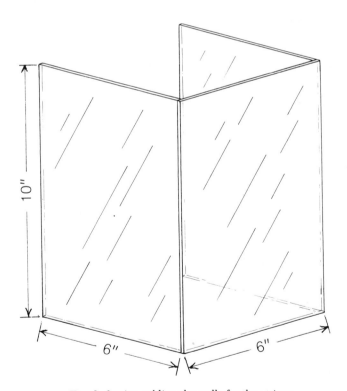

Fig. 3–6   Assembling the walls for the atrium

ADDING EXTERIOR TRIM AND ROOF

The stripping on the exterior of the house and the roof are the two last steps before completion. Paint the balsa strips *before* cutting. The sizes needed are:

thirty-eight 10″-long strips
two 4″ strips
six 3¼″ strips
thirteen 2″ strips

Place the strips at 2-inch intervals all around the house. Naturally, the 10-inch strips are the full-length ones. The others go at appropriate places below the windows. The strips are painted white or any color contrasting with the rest of the house. They may be attached with Elmer's glue.

Before attaching the moldings to the front and rear of the house, paint them the same color as the strips. They may then be glued across both front and back at a height of 10 inches.

The roof is made of Masonite and should be painted with a high-gloss enamel. Cut the roof in half lengthwise and attach the halves with the 1-inch hinges. The roof will rest nicely on the front and rear ends of the house and may be lifted off at any time.

The front door in this house is of Plexiglas, trimmed with decorative tape and shiny brass hinges. The hinges were glued to the Plexiglas with contact cement, then small screws were used to attach them to the house. The door certainly can be made of plywood and painted white. The handle is of paper-covered wire, painted gold and attached with glue.

Your contemporary house is now ready to be landscaped and furnished.

CHAPTER 4 *Spanish Hacienda*

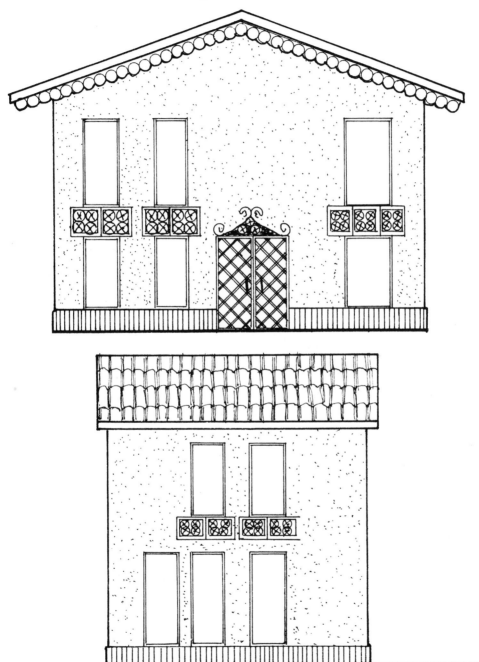

Fig. 4–1   Architect's drawing of exterior, front and side views

MATERIALS REQUIRED

34 square feet of plywood, $3/16''$ seconds	$7.00
One 4′ strip of decorative molding	3.00
One 4′ strip of beading for roof trim	1.00
Two 4′ strips of decorative molding for base of house @ $2 each	4.00
One *good* paintbrush	2.00
Four packs of very coarse sandpaper (three sheets to a pack @ 69¢ a pack; often less expensive if bought by the sheet instead).	3.00
One quart pale pink latex paint	3.00
Large size Elmer's glue	2.00
Door hinges (plastic)	.50
Door hinges (brass)	1.25
55″ or less, depending on ceiling heights, of $3/4''$ corner molding for supports	2.00
Half pint of stain for moldings and floors	.50
Grillwork front door (free scrap from contractor)	—
Plastic for windows	2.00
	$31.25

This Spanish dollhouse is interesting to build, since it is finished with "stucco" and is trimmed with fancy moldings (Figs. 4-1 and 4-2). The grillwork front door is a scrap of radiator cover screening and was cut by a contractor. If wire snips are part of your tool supply, the grillwork can be cut with these. The windows are of heavy plastic, cut from fillers bought for photograph albums, or can be cut from sheet plastic purchased in 2 by 3-foot pieces in a hobby shop.

This house is 32 inches wide, 22 inches deep, and 28 inches high at the peak of the roof.

The actual cost of the wood for this house was about $7. The wood is $3/16$-

Fig. 4–2   Spanish hacienda with stucco exterior

inch second-quality plywood. The reason the cost was so low is that the entire house was built from scraps—leftovers from the lumberyard. One piece that was perfect for the interior walls was free because it had been painted on one side which, of course, made no difference, since the interior of the house is either painted or papered anyway. The heavy decorative molding used at the base of the second-floor windows is very expensive (Fig. 4-2). One 4-foot strip costs $3; fortunately for the pocketbook, one strip is enough.

CUTTING THE PARTS

Once all the supplies have been assembled and a good place to work has been found, construction may be started on the Spanish house and, as always, measuring and cutting are most important. A floor plan is provided in Fig. 4-3; a cutting diagram for all plywood parts is supplied in Figs. 4-4 and 4-5. There is just one word of caution concerning the plywood. If, after the wood is purchased, you find that there just is not going to be any time available to cut it for a few days, be sure to keep the plywood stacked *flat*. Do *not* lean it against a wall because it bends very easily and is difficult to straighten later.

To make the cutting on the front of the house a little easier, the first and second-floor windows are cut as one (Fig. 4-6). When the molding (Fig. 4-7) is placed across the windows, this separates the first and second story of the house, as illustrated.

When the cutting has been completed, but before assembling the house, paint or paper the interior walls. This is so much easier when done before the house is put together. Put the doors on at this time. When cutting the doors, remember to make them a fraction smaller than the opening. When cutting the wood for the second-floor ceiling, cut this $1/2$ inch smaller than the first floor to allow for the $1/4$-inch plywood walls on each end. In this case, since $3/16$-inch plywood was used, the second floor would not be quite $1/2$ inch smaller.

The grill front door should be attached at this time. Before attaching, paint the grillwork and the hinges flat black for a wrought-iron look. The hinges are just plain copper brads. Use four brads on each side, spacing them evenly, and do not hammer all the way in. Leave just a fraction of an inch to allow the door to swing easily. If strap hinges are desired, these can be made from paper-covered wire (the garbage bag twist type) which has been painted black and attached with Weldwood or some other type of epoxy cement. The scrollwork above the front door also can be made from the same paper-covered wire, painted, and attached with glue (Fig. 4-8 gives a pattern for scrollwork). It is extremely important to attack this front door before assembling the house. It can be done much easier working on a flat surface.

The floors can be done at this time, or later when the house is built.

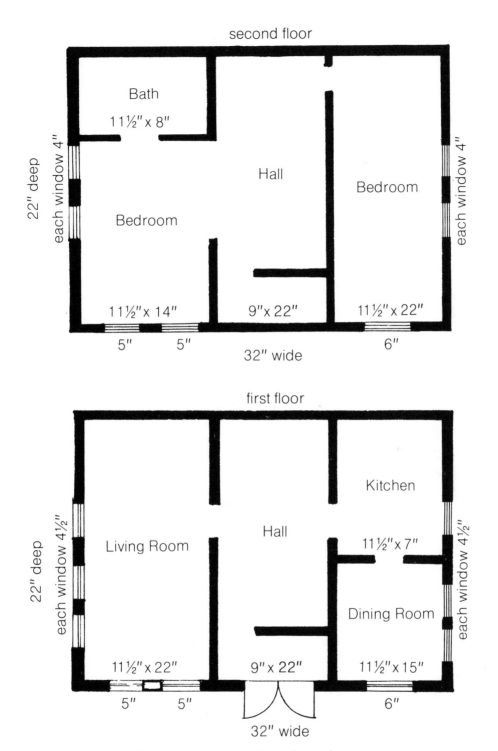

Fig. 4–3   Floor plan for first and second stories

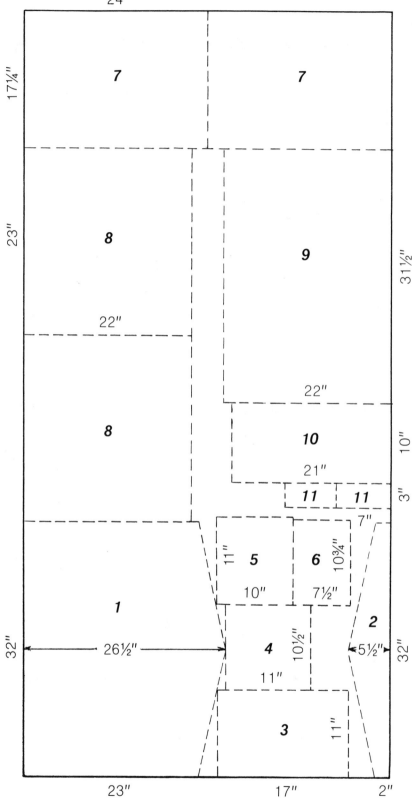

Fig. 4-4 Cutting diagram for plywood pieces

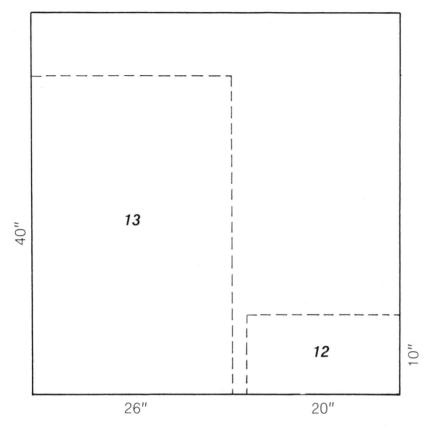

Fig. 4–5   Layout of parts for Spanish house

Sometimes it is a little hard to tell just how a certain type of floor will look until the house is put together.

When staining the exterior moldings, do not forget to stain the ends. The staining is done before putting them on the house.

If heavy plastic is being used for the windows, paint the walls first, since it is difficult to paint over plastic. In this particular case, since the "stucco" has to be applied, it will be simpler to do if the windows have *not* been installed.

APPLYING STUCCO

Stucco the exterior walls *before* assembling the house. It will be much easier to get a smooth job if the sandpaper is applied to a flat surface, rather than a vertical one. More pressure can be applied at the seams to keep them smooth and flat while the glue is drying.

The only materials needed to stucco the house are coarse sandpaper, El-

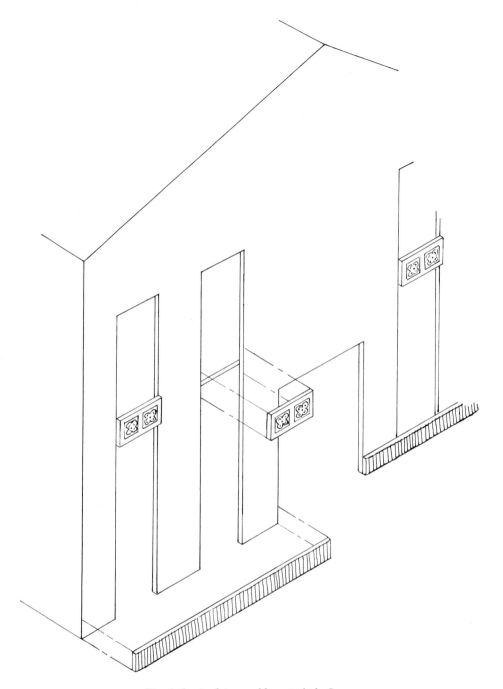

Fig. 4–6 Applying moldings to hide floor

mer's or similar glue, and plenty of single-edged razor blades. Spread the glue evenly on an exterior section of the house, attach the sandpaper as smoothly as possible, and let dry thoroughly. Cover the window spaces as well. It is much less complicated to cut around the windows than to try to measure and cut the

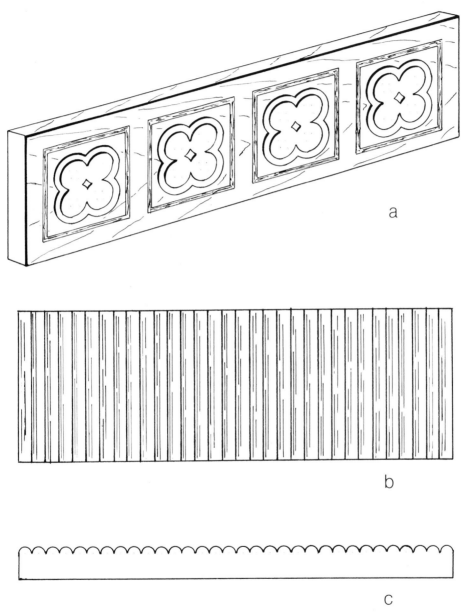

Fig. 4–7 (a) Moldings used to divide first and second stories; (b) molding for base of house; (c) side view of base molding shows depth

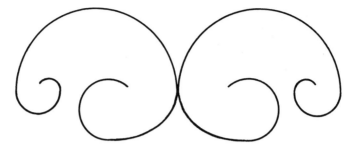

Fig. 4–8   Pattern for scrollwork above front door

paper first. The paper cut from the window spaces will not be wasted; it will be used on another part of the house. Since many smaller pieces will be used, it is important to do the seams as neatly as possible. Coarse sandpaper wears a razor blade down very quickly, which explains the suggestion to have a large supply of blades on hand. Your Spanish house will look very peculiar to you after the sandpaper has been applied, but after the windows are cut and the exterior is painted, the builder should be delighted with the result. Assemble the house according to instructions in chapter 1, then paint. Spray paint can be used, but regular interior latex wall paint was used on the house here (see color Fig. 3). A good paintbrush is extremely important for use in the painting of the "stucco." The course sandpaper tends to pull at the bristles and, if a cheap brush is used, the housepainter will go out of his mind trying to remove the loose bristles from the wet paint.

Once the exterior has been painted and after it has been allowed to dry, there is now one more step before installing the windows.

If the seams in the stucco are too obvious after the paint has dried, this can be taken care of without too much trouble. Apply a *very* thin coat of Elmer's glue to the seams and, while the glue is still wet (just a little tacky), sprinkle fine sand over the glue and let dry. After this has dried, paint the seams, and they should not be visible. The seams can be disguised with vines, espaliered trees, and other exterior plantings.

FINISHING THE EXTERIOR

If wallpaper was not hung before the house was assembled, measure the paper before putting in the windows. It is very difficult to apply wallpaper and trim it neatly around the windows after the panes are in. If moldings are desired, these can be put on after the windows are installed and, in fact, will cover the rough edges of the plastic which is on top of the wallpaper. Wooden moldings can be made from very thin strips of balsa, painted and glued on. Most commercially manufactured dollhouses have painted moldings on the windows. There is still an easier way to have extremely effective moldings that look much

better than painted ones and are simpler to do than carved ones. These moldings come from a fabric shop and are braids of the proper width—which means
whatever size you desire—and then are painted. After the paint has dried, just
glue them on.

If heavy plastic is used for the windows, there is an easy way to measure
and cut. Because the plastic is difficult to see while marking, and since most
pens and pencils will not write on plastic, take a piece of construction paper the
same size as the page of plastic. Draw the window on the *paper*, then cut both
the paper and plastic at the same time. If the interior painting and papering and
the stuccoing of the exterior have been completed, the windows now may be installed. Windows can go in either before or after assembling the house. It is a
little more difficult after the house is together, but preferable to taking a chance
of knocking them out while hammering.

When the exterior paint has dried, the decorative moldings may be attached. Use a good strong contact cement such as Weldwood, and follow the directions on the tube or bottle. C clamps will not be needed, providing the
plywood was kept flat and did not warp before use.

MAKING THE ROOF

This type of house should have a tile roof. Unfortunately, the best material
for Spanish tiles was old-fashioned corrugated cardboard which could be pasted
to the plywood roof and then painted the orange-red of real Spanish tiles. The
old-fashioned corrugated cardboard is practically nonexistent, so this roof is
plain plywood with painted tiles. The 1/2-inch beading, stained and glued to the
edge of the roof, gives the house a finished look (Fig. 4-9). In this case, the trim
was attached only to the front of the roof in order to save money, but it certainly
can be put all around the roof and would look very nice.

COMPLETING THE INTERIOR

When finishing the floors, there is a very painless way to make superb tile.
First, find some embossed wallpaper—wallpaper with a smooth, raised design of
either small circles or squares. Paint the paper any color you wish, then paint
with Mod-Podge to give it a real tile effect. Mod-Podge is a product used for

Fig. 4–9 Beading for roof trim, actual size

sealing decoupage and is made by Connoisseur Studio, Inc., Box 7187, Louis-ville, Kentucky 40207. This can be found in many hobby or craft shops. Several coats of this lacquer will give such a realistic tile floor, it will be hard to distin-guish from real tile even when it is touched. Be sure to allow enough drying time between coats to avoid stickiness.

The stairs are completed after the floors, since the steps come into the hall and it is better not to have to do the floor around them. The stairs are *not* the same 1:12 scale as the rest of the house. Because this particular house has 11-foot ceilings downstairs, the decision reached by the three builders was that a slightly larger staircase was more effective. However, if one wants to keep the house perfectly to scale, the method of building the stairs is exactly the same. Take a piece of plywood and draw the side pieces, as shown in Fig. 4-10. Next, on a piece of balsa wood $1/8$ inch thick, draw the steps or treadboards. The side pieces are $15^3/4$ inches long and $1^5/8$ inches wide. The treadboards are 1 inch deep and $4^1/4$ inches wide. This staircase was made without risers to avoid a heavy feeling. After cutting, stain or paint all the parts of the staircase before putting it together. If one side of the staircase is glued to the hall wall, this will support the opposite side. It is not necessary to cut the sides for the staircase yourself. For a long staircase this is time consuming and difficult. Sides can be ordered from dollhouse catalogues and are very inexpensive—75¢ for 3 feet.

If you want a fireplace, a real masonry one can be built using the same basic principles as the one for the log cabin in Chapter 2. To adjust the size, make the basic balsa-wood box smaller or larger. Small colored chips, such as those used in aquariums and for flower bulbs, may be set in the mortar. Fire-places may be bought, or a wooden fireplace may be made with little effort. Start with three pieces of wood about an inch thick and whatever height or width you choose. By adding moldings, as shown in Figure 4-11, the fireplace and mantel may be made as plain or elaborate as one desires.

If the builder of this house has an urge for a stained-glass window, it is not difficult to achieve. Colored cellophane cut into various shapes can be glued to the plastic window, using black construction paper for the "lead" that holds it together. Greeting cards are a good source of supply for stained glass. Many such cards are decorated with plastic stained glass heavy enough to be used just as it is. Plastic stained glass is also available in craft shops. This is about the same thickness as the Plexiglas windows used in the log cabin and the contem-porary house. This Plexiglas is $1/16$ inch thick.

The Spanish house is ready for furnishing.

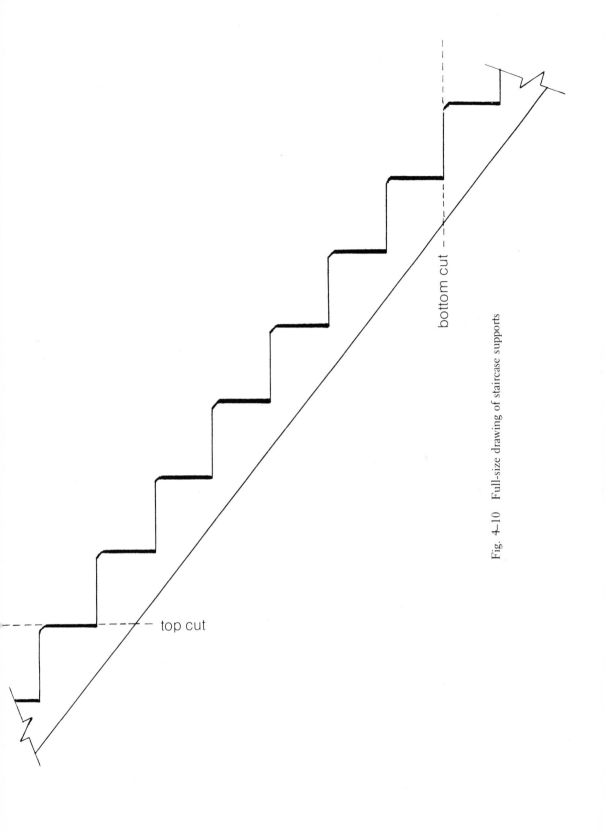

top cut

bottom cut

Fig. 4-10 Full-size drawing of staircase supports

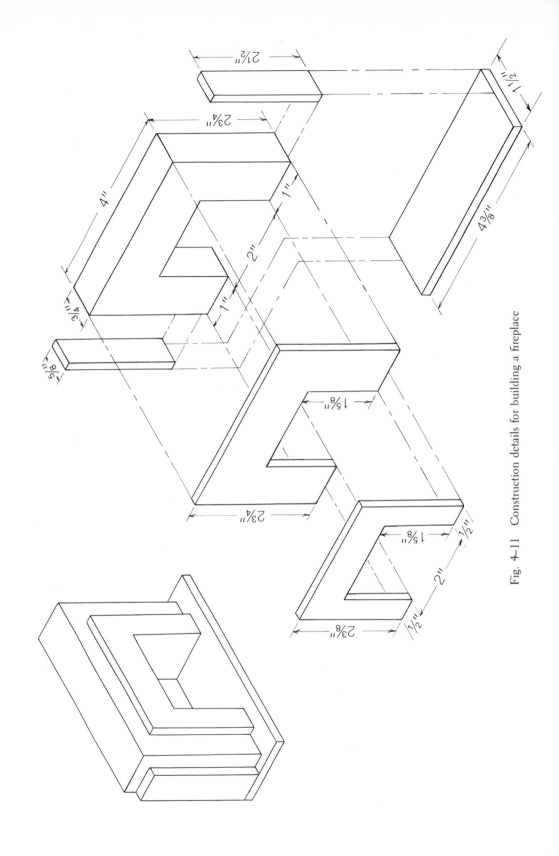

Fig. 4-11 Construction details for building a fireplace

CHAPTER 5 *Plantation House*

Fig. 5–1   Architect's drawing of front of southern mansion

MATERIALS REQUIRED

Two sheets of 4′ × 8′ *second*-quality ³/₈″ plywood at $7	$14.00
Two dowels, 36″ long and 1″ in diameter	.75
Four 36″ strips of ¹/₄″-square balsa @ .30	1.20
Two sheets of balsa, 4″ wide, ¹/₈″ thick, and 36″ long to make shutters @ .75	1.50
12′ of balsa ¹/₈″ wide for window mullions	.75
Five sets of small brass hinges (six per package) @ .69	1.25
Two pairs of 1″ hinges for each side of roof	.50
Two paintbrushes	2.00
One quart latex paint for exterior	3.50
Half pint of stain for floors	.50
Pint of dark green enamel for shutters and roof	1.00
Half pint of red paint for "brick" porch	.50
Felt-tip pen to do "bricks"	.25
Material for stairs	2.50
	$30.20

The plantation house or southern mansion is the largest of all the doll-houses in this book (Figs. 5-1 to 5-3 and color Fig. 4). It is 36 inches wide, 24 inches deep, and 28 inches high at the peak of the roof. There is a balcony which runs the entire width of the house and there is a brick front porch.

This house as it stands took two 4 by 8-foot pieces of $^3/_8$-inch plywood to build. Of course, the base can be reduced, leaving just room for the porch, which is 5 inches deep.

There is brick flooring paper made to scale for dollhouses. The flooring looks real and was used on the porch of this house. An 11 by 14-inch piece of

Fig. 5–2   Back of the finished plantation house showing interior

Fig. 5–3   Southern mansion with balcony running the full length of the front

Fig. 1 Authentic
log cabin
replica

Fig. 2 Contemporary house
with atrium

g. 3 Spanish hacienda
with
stucco exterior

Fig. 4   Southern mansion
with columns and balcony

Fig. 5   Victorian house
with gingerbread trim

Fig. 6   New England
saltbox,
designed in 1670s

Fig. 7   Restored Edwardian dollhouse

Fig. 8   Replica of a house
in the Germantown section
of Philadelphia

Fig. 10   Handmade contemporary
A-frame house

Fig. 9   Victorian house
with sides that open
to reveal interior

Fig. 11 Showcase house for
miniature display

Fig. 12 Interior of the
Edwardian dollhouse in Fig. 7

Fig. 13 Stucco farmhouse, c. 1890

this flooring is 75¢. The porch and front walk require one and a half pieces of this paper, which would be $1.50—not that much more than the cost of the paint mentioned in the materials list. There should be enough white latex to paint the interior of the house, and two or three packages of gift-wrap paper at 50¢ each will more than take care of the wallpapering. So, for a very modest cost, a very good and sturdy dollhouse can be built.

MEASURING AND CUTTING

To begin construction on this house, as with all the dollhouses, the measuring and drawing of each section of the plywood is the first step. The floor plans are supplied in Fig. 5-4. The patterns shown in Figs. 5-5 and 5-6 are designed to keep the amount of plywood needed to a minimum. The key explaining the cutting diagrams is as follows.

Figure 5-5

1. Front: 36″ wide, 27³/4″ high at peak, 19¹/2″ at sides
2. Back: same dimensions as front, except that a piece of wood 18¹/2″ is cut out—this cut is made 9″ below the peak
3. Second-floor room partition: 13³/4″ × 13³/4″ × 7¹/2″ × 15″
4. Two first-floor room partitions the same size, each 3″ × 11¹/2″
5. Seven doors, each 3″ × 6³/4″
6. Two sides, each 24″ × 19¹/2″
7. Two first-floor hall partitions, 11¹/2″ × 23³/4″
8. Two second-floor hall partitions, each 23″ × 13³/4″
9. Two roof sections (one section in Fig. 5-6), each 26″ × 21″

Figure 5-6

10. Second floor, 35¹/2″ × 23¹/4″
11. Balcony, 35¹/2″ × 3³/4″
12. Base, 36″ × 48″

After the measuring has been completed, cutting will be the next step, hopefully with a power saw. The difficult part of the cutting is the windows. If it is feasible to spend a little more money, especially if a power saw has to be rented for this, take the plywood with the measurements accurately drawn on it, and any lumberyard workman, builder, or carpenter will do the entire cutting job for $4 or $5. The cost of cutting the Spanish dollhouse was $4—less than it would cost to rent a power saw for a couple of days. It is remarkable, too, to see the contrast between cutting done by an amateur and that of a professional. When the pro does it, there is not a chance of having a crooked window, or a

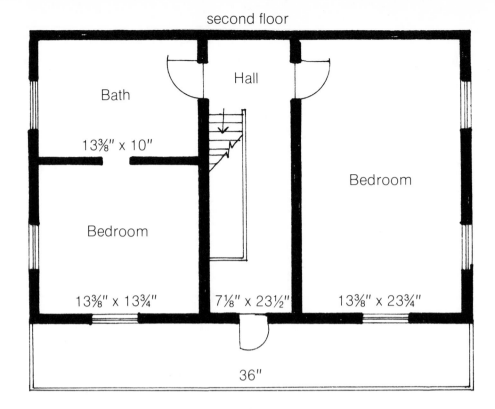

second floor

Bath

13⅜" x 10"

Hall

Bedroom

Bedroom

13⅜" x 13¾"   7⅛" x 23½"   13⅜" x 23¾"

36"

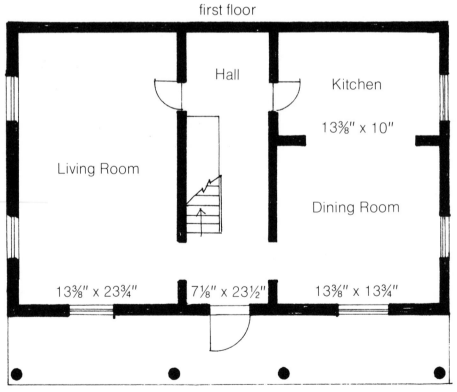

first floor

Hall

Kitchen

13⅜" x 10"

Living Room

Dining Room

13⅜" x 23¾"   7⅛" x 23½"   13⅜" x 13¾"

Fig. 5–4   Floor plan for the two stories

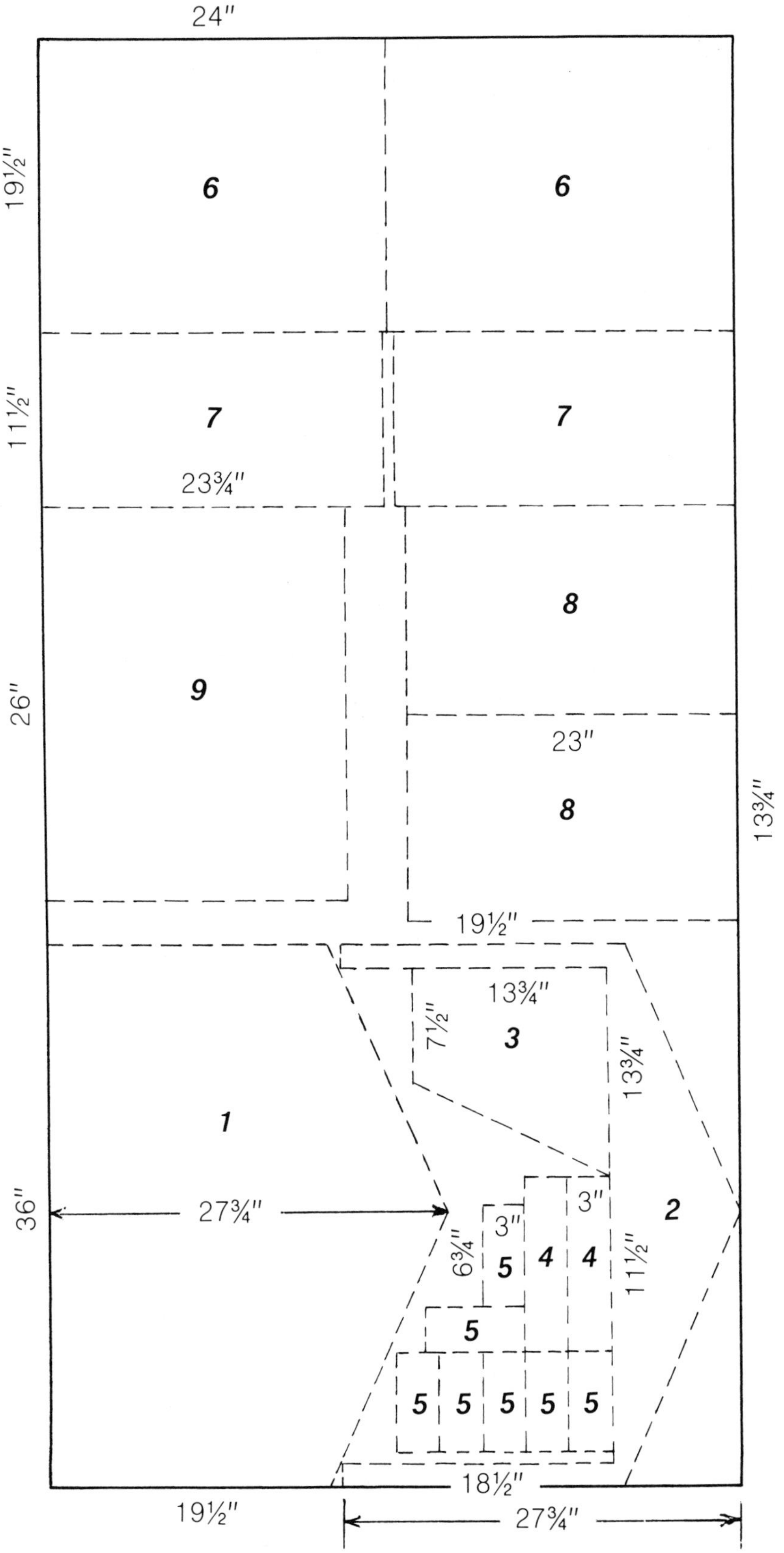

Fig. 5–5 Layout for cutting plywood

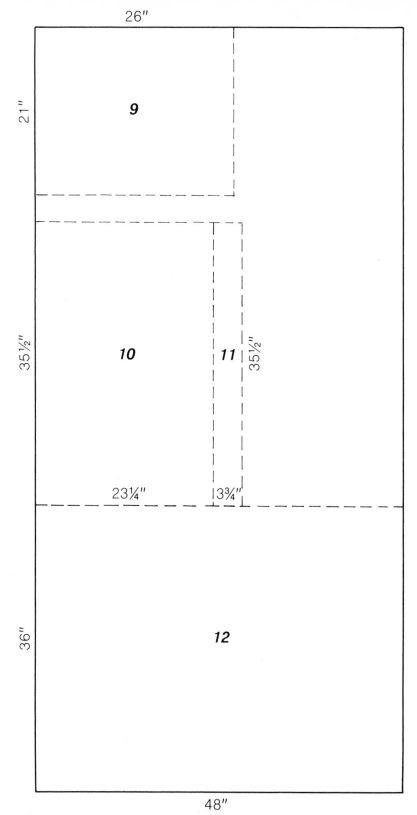

Fig. 5–6 Cutting diagram for plywood parts

crooked anything else for that matter. Be sure to shop around for prices first. Some people may charge twice as much as others.

When building this or any of the dollhouses, remember on the interior wall sizes to allow for the $3/8$-inch plywood, which would subtract $3/16$ inch from each wall. Therefore, the room sizes will not be precisely the dimensions on the original plans. All rooms will be $3/8$ inch smaller, but if you total the number of eighth inches used on inside walls, the measurements will equal the original plan. Assemble the house following the procedure in chapter 1.

ADDING A BALLROOM AND ROOF

A ballroom was not uncommon in a plantation house. If you want to include one, it will not be necessary to change any of the cutting of the sides or back of the house. The only changes will be to cut a third floor the same size as the second and to lower the ceiling height of the second floor rooms to $7^1/2$ inches. The third floor can be left divided into rooms, as it now would be if second-floor ceilings were installed, or interior walls can be cut away at ceiling level to provide the ballroom (Fig. 5-7). In order for the $3/8$-inch plywood not to go above the top edge of the house, the height of the doors should be lowered $1/4$ inch, so that the wall height on the second floor can be lowered $1/4$ inch.

The roof actually rests on the pediments at the front and rear of the house. The hinges are attached to each side piece of the roof itself, as shown in Figs. 5-8 and 5-9. Using this method, the entire roof may be removed easily.

Fig. 5-10 shows a strip of wood approximately 1 inch wide and $1/2$ inch thick that is nailed to the top of the front and rear pediments of the house to give support if a ballroom is added and there are no third-floor supporting walls.

If you prefer a stationary roof, one which is not removable but has sides that can be lifted, this is built in the following ways: Take two strips of wood, each about 1 inch wide, $1/4$ inch thick and long enough to reach between the pediments at the top of the house. Nail each strip to the front and rear pediment on each side to form the "tip" of the roof, running the length of the house. This "triangle" actually will be the top of the roof on each side. The roof will be attached to the strip on each side (Fig. 5-11). Hinges will be used as before. The only difference is that the roof is permanently attached to the top of the house instead of being removable. The sides will lift. Naturally, the side of the roof will have to be shortened to allow for the piece of wood at the top to which it is attached.

Fig. 5-7 Installation of the third floor to create a ballroom

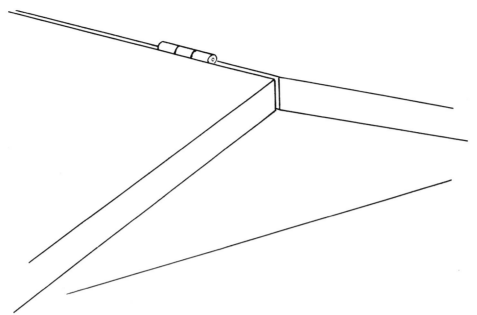

Fig. 5–8   Drawing of hinged roof

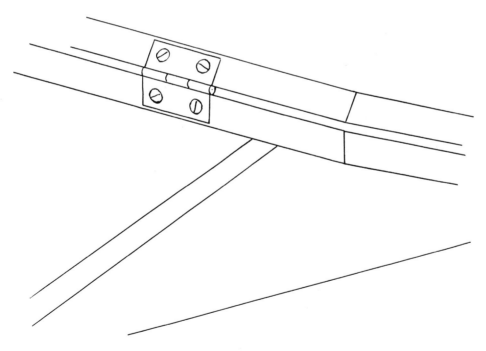

Fig. 5–9   Underside of hinged roof

59

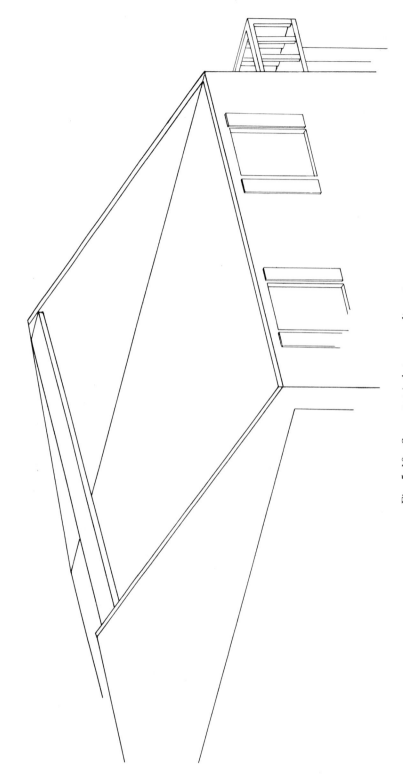

Fig. 5–10   Support strip between pediments

Fig. 5–11   Hinged roof is permanently attached to support strips at peak

ERECTING THE BALCONY

After the plantation house has been built, this is the time to add the balcony. The balcony is 3³/₄ inches deep and 35¹/₂ inches wide, running almost the entire width of the house. The edge of the balcony can be glued to the front of the house with contact cement; the balcony floor is then supported by the four columns, spaced 11 inches apart, starting 1¹/₄ inches from the end of the balcony and 1¹/₄ inches from the front, measuring from the center of the column. The dowel columns are fastened by screwing through the balcony floor and into the dowel centers. The columns are 11¹/₄ inches high and 1 inch in diameter; the bottoms of the columns can be screwed or glued to the porch base, or both.

The most difficult part is the railing around the balcony. There are three ways to do this railing: One is the way it is shown in Fig. 5-12, using 14 feet of ¹/₄-inch-square balsa. The second way is to buy iron fencing at $1.70 per 2¹/₂ inches, which would cost about $28. This method, obviously, would be prohibitive for most. The third choice is probably not only the the simplest, but the least expensive (although it would be "fudging" somewhat on the design of the house). Take decorative Masonite—the kind used for cupboards and room dividers—as shown in Fig. 5-13. Cut as shown in Fig. 5-14. This can be glued to the balcony with contact cement.

Fig. 5–12 Balcony and railing constructed of balsa

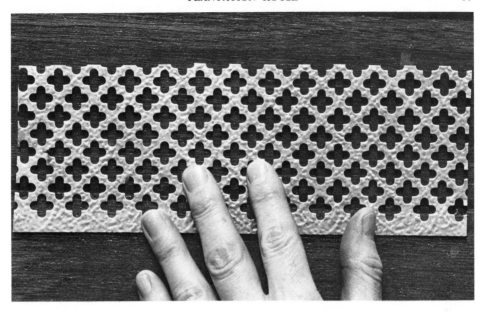

Fig. 5–13   Masonite molding, optionally used for railing

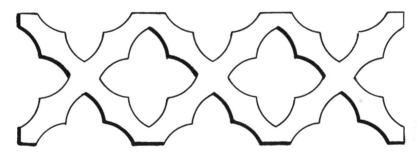

Fig. 5–14   Cutting the Masonite railing

If the $1/4$-inch balsa is used for the balcony, the top railing should be 3 inches high from the floor, including the base railing. There should be 1 inch of space between the spindles. There are thirty-two spindles, each $2^1/2$ inches high. The only two spindles that are placed differently are the two side ones closest to the front railing (see Fig. 5-12). These two are only $1/2$ inch from the corner front spindles.

FINISHING THE MANSION

The doors are 3 by $6^3/4$ inches, the windows are 3 by 6 inches. To make the shutters for the windows, take one 36-inch-long piece of balsa, 4 inches

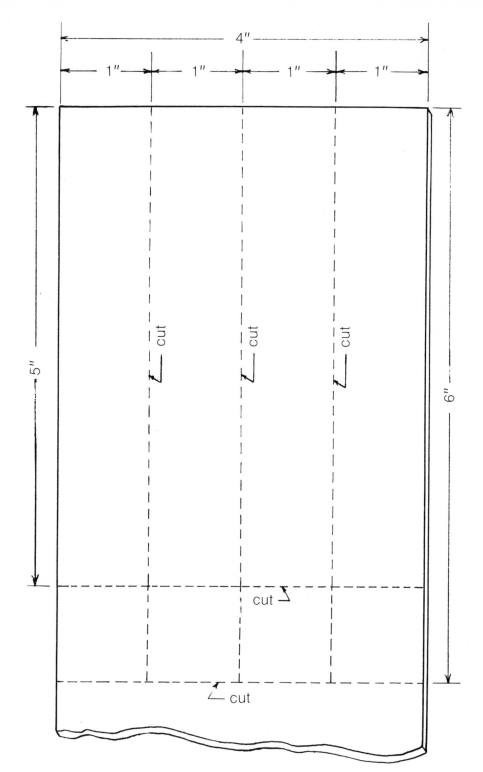

Fig. 5-15   Full-size shutter pattern

wide, and measure four 1-inch shutters across, 6 inches long (Fig. 5-15). Measure the windows before cutting the mullions or stripping from the $1/16$-inch balsa. The mullions should be $1/8$ inch wide (Fig. 5-16). Paint the mullions white before installing them in the windows.

The entire house should be painted before installing the windows. While the white paint is drying, the roof and shutters may be painted dark green. After the white paint has dried thoroughly, the shutters may be attached, using Elmer's glue. If the shutters tend to slip before the glue is dry, they may be held in place with a small pin.

There is "shingle" paper available for roofing which is made to the same scale as the "brick" used for the porch. However, the roof of this house is so large that the cost of the "shingle" paper would be considerably more than the cost of a half pint of paint. The shingle papers are not nearly as realistic as the brick papers. The plantation house is now ready for landscaping and interior decoration.

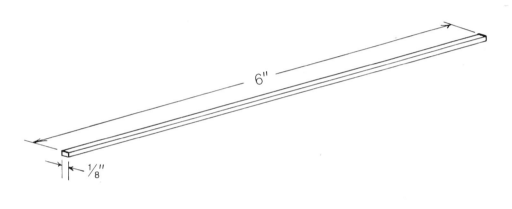

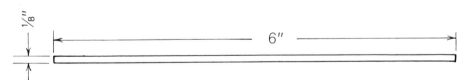

Fig. 5–16   Making mullions to complete window trim

CHAPTER 6 *Victorian Mansion*

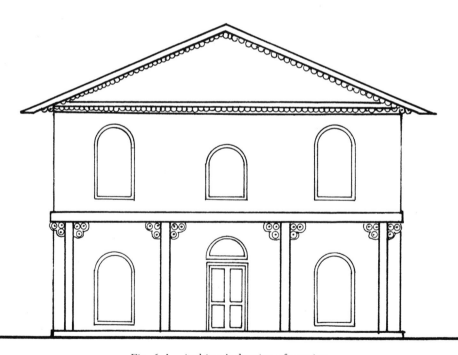

Fig. 6–1   Architect's drawing of exterior

MATERIALS REQUIRED

Two pieces of 4' × 8' plywood, 3/8" thick (only one and one-half pieces will be used)	$14.00
One dowel, 36" long, 1" in diameter	.50
Gingerbread trim—one piece of molding 6' long	3.00
Porch railing—1/4"-square balsa, 25" long	.50
39" of 1/8" × 1" stripping to go around edge of porch roof	.50
Seven sets of 1" brass hinges for doors at 69¢ per pair	5.00
Two sets of 1" hinges for roof if it is not nailed	1.50
Heavy plastic for windows—two 2' × 3' sheets	1.50
"Stained glass" above front door (free or from a bought greeting card)	—
One pint of paint for exterior	1.00
Half pint of paint for trim	.50
Half pint of enamel for house roof and porch roof	.50
Half pint of wood stain for floors	.50
Material for stairs	2.00
	$31.00

The Victorian house is great fun to build. The exterior of this version is a combination of two real houses of the Victorian era. One of the houses which was partially copied is painted the same shade of blue with white trim (Figs. 6-1, 6-2, and color Fig. 5). The porch and trim were taken from one house and the window designs from another. This can be built with or without the porch railing.

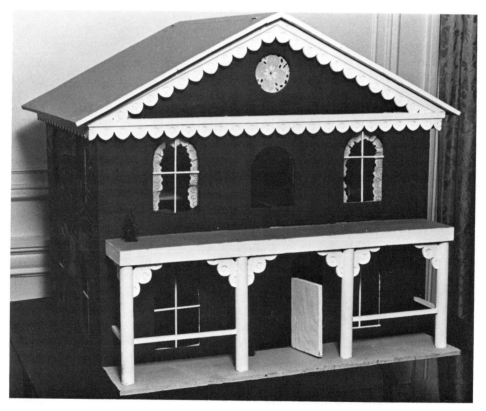

Fig. 6–2   Victorian dollhouse with gingerbread trim

This house measures 30 inches wide, 24 inches deep, and 28 inches high to the peak of the roof. The base is 30 by 42 inches. The porch extends 5 inches from the front of the house and is 29 inches wide. The Victorian house can be cut by 2 inches on the sides and front without spoiling the lines and, except for allowing enough base for the porch, unless you plan to plant shrubbery, the wide base is not necessary.

The materials needed for this house are listed with the costs. The amount of plywood here is for the *maximum*-size house, as shown in the floor plans (Fig. 6-3). Naturally, if the size of the house is reduced and there is no 6-inch base on three sides, then less plywood will be needed.

BUILDING OPTIONS

The cost of the interior finish, except for staining the floors, is not included because the interior walls can be done in so many different ways. For instance, most Victorian houses have in the front hall either elaborately patterned wallpaper or dark-stained paneling or paper above the paneling. For the dark walls, one could use the same stain as that for the floors. If moldings are desired, balsa strips make fine moldings for only a few cents.

If you want fireplaces, they can be bought through catalogues, starting in price at about $4.50, or can be made for practically nothing, using about 14 inches of 1-inch-square pine (see Fig. 4-11). This allows for a 4-inch mantel, 5 inches high. Naturally, a fireplace can be made as elaborate as you please for very little cost by adding moldings, or they can be made with Sacrete, as shown in Figs. 2-12 and 2-13. If true realism is wanted, then a chimney may be attached to the roof just by cutting a block of wood approximately 3 inches square, the desired height, and angling the bottom to fit smoothly to the roof (Fig. 6-4). It is not necessary to do any complicated measuring to get the correct angle. Take the block of wood, hold it straight up against the edge of the roof, and draw a line on the wood showing the slope of the roof.

Using two 1-inch hinges, the roof may be attached to a center molding which runs the entire depth of the house, as shown in Figs. 5-8 through 5-11. This molding is attached with nails to the peak at both front and back. Remember, though, if this method of attaching the roof is used, the actual sides of the roof will be correspondingly shorter—depending on the length of the molding at the top. Each side of the roof may be hinged together with two 1-inch hinges if you want to have the entire roof removable. When the roof is hinged to the peak, of course, each side may be opened separately to be able to look down into the house.

second floor

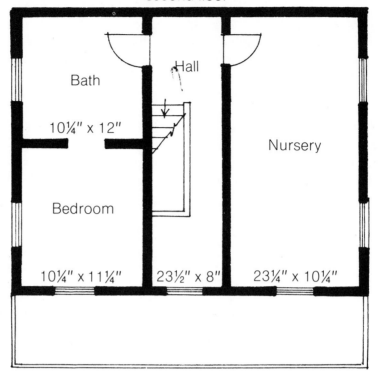

Bath

10¼" x 12"

Hall

Nursery

Bedroom

10¼" x 11¼"   23½" x 8"   23¼" x 10¼"

first floor

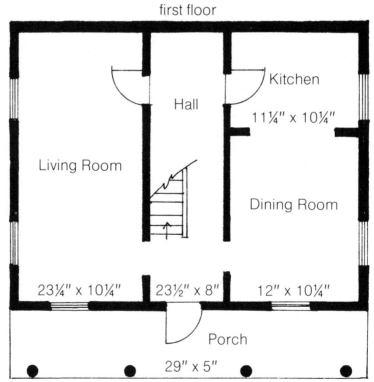

Kitchen

Hall   11¼" x 10¼"

Living Room

Dining Room

23¼" x 10¼"   23½" x 8"   12" x 10¼"

Porch

29" x 5"

Fig. 6–3   Floor plan for first and second stories

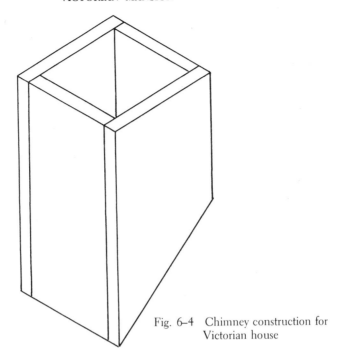

Fig. 6–4   Chimney construction for
Victorian house

MEASURING AND MARKING

Because of the rounded windows, it is a good idea to have the parts for this house cut professionally. By measuring very carefully and drawing on the plywood every single door and window that you want cut, as shown in Fig. 6-5 and 6-6, it will take a surprisingly short time for a pro to do this cutting. As mentioned before, this cost can be kept to $4 or $5, but since professionals charge by the hour, the more measuring and drawing done by the builder, the less the charge by the cutter.

There are fifteen windows; the measurements for the windows and doors are marked on each applicable piece after the outline is drawn on the plywood. Four of the front windows are 4 by 6 inches; they are 4½ inches from each side, 1 inch from the bottom of the house, and 2 inches from the top of the second story—the same level as the side windows. The center second-story window is 4 by 5 inches; the stained-glass window above the front door is a semicircle, 4 inches wide and 1½ inches high. The round center window at the top of the house is 3 inches in diameter and 2 inches below the peak of the roof. The side windows are 4 by 6 inches and are placed 4 inches from the front, 3½ inches from the back, 1 inch from the bottom, and 2 inches from the top. The front door is 4 by 6 inches, and the interior doors are 3 by 6 inches.

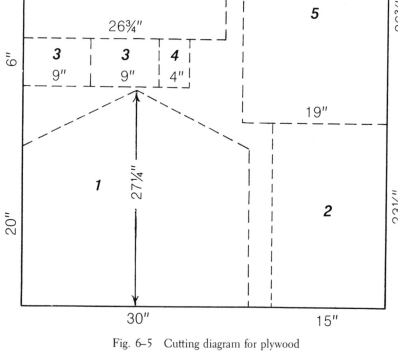

Fig. 6–5   Cutting diagram for plywood

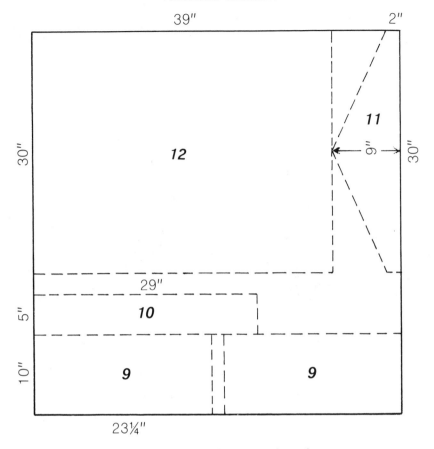

Fig. 6–6   Pattern for cutting plywood

Figure 6-5

1. Front: 30″ wide, 20″ high at sides, and 27¼″ at peak of roof
2. Upstairs hall partition (need 2): 15″ × 23¼″
3. Room partition (need 2): 6″ × 9″
4. Front door: 4″ × 6″
5. Roof (need 2): 19″ × 26¾″
6. Second floor: 29¼″ × 23¼″
7. Interior door (need 4): 3″ × 6″
8. Side (need 2): 24″ × 20″

Figure 6-6

9. Downstairs hall partitions (need 2): 10″ × 23¼″
10. Porch roof: 29″ × 5″
11. Back: 30″ wide, 2″ at sides, and 9″ at peak
12. Base: 30″ × 39″

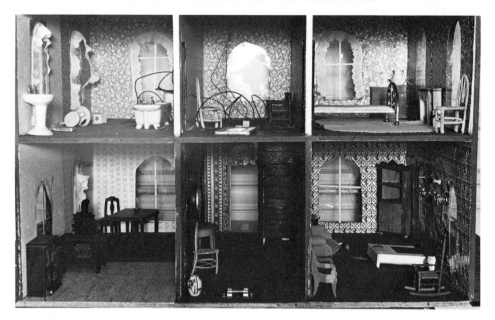

Fig. 6–7   Interior of Victorian dollhouse with room partitions removed; house is in the process of being wired

The base extension was reduced from 6 inches to 3 inches on each side to keep within the one and one-half sheets of plywood; if the wider base is desired, then two sheets of plywood will be needed.

After the house has been cut and is ready for assembly, it is much easier to attach all doors, and paint, paper, or stain each room before putting the house together. Do *not* put the "glass" in the windows until after the exterior has been painted. Assemble the house as indicated in the instructions in chapter 1 (completed interior is shown in Fig. 6-7.)

TRIMMING THE EXTERIOR

When attaching the gingerbread trim to the Victorian house, be sure to paint all the trim first. With molding such as this, shown in Fig. 6-8, spraying the paint rather than brushing it on may be preferred, since it is difficult to get into the small places with a brush (a watercolor brush is too soft). After the paint has dried thoroughly, nail a strip of wood $1/2$ inch wide and $1/2$ inch thick (which has also been painted the same color as the molding) across all parts of the house to which the trim will be attached. Then, nail the gingerbread to the $1/2$-inch-thick strip. Having the trim set out slightly from the house, rather than being right against it, gives a much more realistic look (Figs. 6-9 and 6-11).

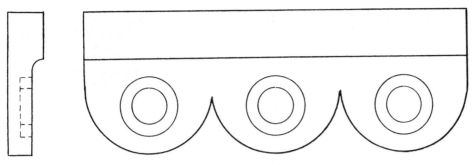

Fig. 6–8   Drawing of gingerbread molding, actual size

Another material that makes excellent "gingerbread" is Masonite trim which is used for room dividers or cabinet fronts (see Figs. 5-13 and 5-14). Saw one width of pattern the length that is needed and use this for the trim.

The round window at the top front of the house may be left plain, may be "leaded" using *very* small strips of black construction paper, or may be filled in with lace as shown in color Fig. 5, the completed Victorian house. The mullions for the windows are cut from balsa wood ⅛-inch wide, painted white, and put on after the windows have been installed. The house is now finished.

Fig. 6–9   Rounded windows and unpainted gingerbread trim

Fig. 6–10   Stained-glass window above door

Fig. 6–11   Molding is cut to trim porch; lace shows in window of completed house to create
curtains

CHAPTER 7 *New England Saltbox*

Fig. 7–1   Architect's drawing, front and side of house

MATERIALS REQUIRED

One piece of 4' × 8' plywood, ³/₈" thick	$ 7.00
One pair of ³/₄" hinges for front door	.75
One pair of 1" loose pin hinges for roof	1.00
20" of balsa wood, ¹/₈" thick and 4" wide	1.50
One strip of wood, 1¹/₂" × ³₄" × 30"	.50
One piece heavy plastic, 2' × 3'	.75
One pint barn-red latex paint	2.00
Half pint gray paint for roof	1.00
Half pint white paint for shutters and window stripping	1.00
Several (to allow for mistakes) strips of *very* thin balsa to make mullions for windows, at 10¢ per strip	.50
Felt-tip pen	.50
Dollhouse wallpaper in brick pattern (one sheet)	.75
Paintbrushes	2.00
Staircase supports	.75
Single-edge razor blades	.50
	$20.50

The exterior of the New England Saltbox, shown in Figs. 7-1 and 7-2 and color Fig. 6, is as authentic as it can be for a dollhouse. The interior is copied from an original saltbox but, obviously, can be rearranged by installing plywood panels for room dividers. With the modern kitchen, shown in Fig. 7-3, this house is for living in the 1970s with a floor plan from the 1670s. It proves the old theory that good design is timeless.

The house is 30 inches wide, 22 inches deep, and 23 inches high. The chimney is $3^1/4$ inches square, 6 inches high on the front roof, and $3^1/2$ inches on the back. The windows are 3 by 5 inches, and there is a 6-inch base around

Fig. 7–2 New England saltbox, c. 1670

80

Fig. 7–3   Modern kitchen for 1970s living

three sides of the house. This house can be built from one 4 by 8-foot piece of plywood, ³/₈ inch thick.

To the materials list, add another dollar or two for the interior stains and paint and two or three dollars if dollhouse flooring and wallpaper are used. An 11 by 14-inch sheet of flooring costs 75¢. If gift-wrapping paper is bought for the walls, two dollars should cover that cost. The eagle above the door is a kitchen magnet which cost 25¢.

Real dollhouse windows may be purchased, but they are very expensive. One package of ten windows costs $2.49. For this house, one and one-half packages were required, since these windows are not standard commercial doll-house size. Even if the most expensive materials are used to build this house, the cost still can be kept to less than $30.

MEASURING AND CUTTING

Measuring correctly before putting the saw to the wood is, of course, all important; once a window or door has been cut, there is no way to "un-cut." If

second floor

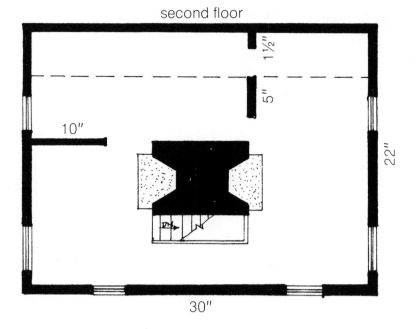

first floor

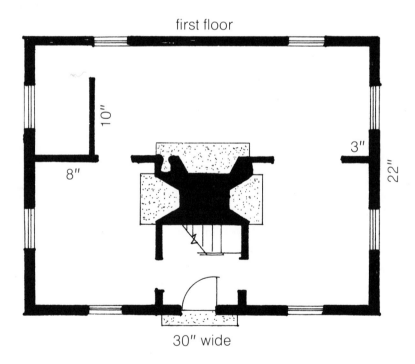

Fig. 7–4　Floor plans for first and second stories

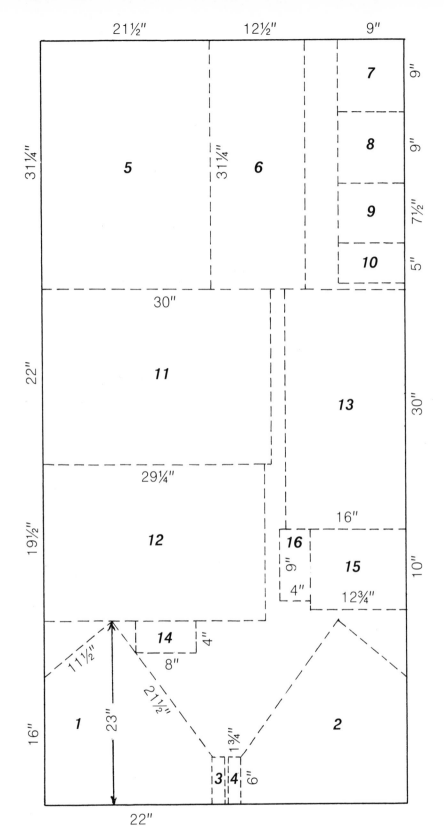

Fig. 7–5   Cutting diagram for plywood parts

the floor plans in Fig. 7-4 and the cutting diagram (Fig. 7-5), for which the key is given below, are followed precisely, there is no reason that the saltbox house you build will not look exactly as the one shown in color Fig. 6.

(Left and right are facing house)

1. Right Side: $16'' \times 22'' \times 11^1/2'' \times 21^1/2'' \times 6''$
2. Left Side: $16'' \times 22'' \times 11'' \times 21^1/2'' \times 6''$
3. Right back: $1^3/4'' \times 6''$
4. Left back: $1^3/4'' \times 6''$
5. Roof rear: $31^1/4'' \times 21^1{}_2''$
6. Roof front: $31^1{}_4'' \times 12^1/2''$ (1″ longer than side pieces 1 and 2 to provide roof overhang)
7. First-floor stairwell: $9'' \times 9''$
8. First-floor left wall partition: $9'' \times 9''$
9. First-floor kitchen wall partition: $9'' \times 7^1/2''$
10. First-floor stairwell: $9'' \times 5''$
11. Base (first floor): $30'' \times 22''$
12. Second floor: $29^1/4'' \times 19^1/2''$
13. Front: $16'' \times 30''$
14. Door: $4'' \times 8''$
15. Second-floor partition: $12^3/4'' \times 10''$
16. First-floor right wall partition: $4'' \times 9''$

PREPARING PARTS FOR ASSEMBLY

It is easy enough to paint the outside of the house after assembling it, but it is much easier to paint or paper the inside before the house is put together. However, it is a good idea to paint the exterior around the windows before they are installed. The rest of the exterior can be left until the house is built (Fig. 7-6). The windows should be installed *after* painting the interior, but if wallpaper is used, the windows should be put in *before* papering. If the plan is to paper the walls, put the paper on the flat surface and draw a pattern of the windows on the paper before putting in the windows. Then, when the time comes to paper the walls, no trimming will be necessary.

When the interior has been completed, before assembling the entire house, prepare all the extras, so when the time comes to put the whole house together, each part will be finished, and no more figuring and cutting will be necessary.

The front door should be painted at this time. Other extras include such things as making the shutters from balsa wood. If 4-inch-wide balsa is used as recommended, then four 1-inch-wide shutters may be cut at a time. Sixteen shutters, 5 inches long, will be needed. Take a ruler and draw them on the balsa wood, as shown in Fig. 5-13. Use a razor blade to cut or an X-acto knife—a kitchen knife is more difficult to use. Cut all the shutters at once. At

Fig. 7–6 Assembled, unpainted house

Fig. 7–7 Painted house with windows, shutters, and mullions in place

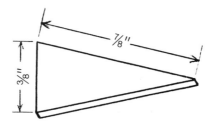

Fig. 7–8   Making a door from ¹/₁₆-inch balsa

the same time, cut the window mullions from balsa ¹/₁₆ inch thick and approximately ¹/₈ inch wide. See Fig. 7-7 of finished house with mullions and shutters in place. The hinges for the front door were cut from ¹/₁₆-inch balsa. Naturally, these are not real working hinges. They are for looks only. The drawing in Fig. 7-8 is exact size. After all the window shutters and trim have been cut, then paint everything white at the same time, using latex paint. The door hinges are to be painted flat black. The door handle is made from paper-covered wire and painted black. It is now time to assemble the whole house.

CONSTRUCTING THE HOUSE

The first-floor room dividers obviously support the second floor, so these should be installed on the base after exterior walls are assembled. The staircase should be put in before the second floor. Although it is entirely possible to cut the supports for the staircase oneself (see Fig. 4-10), it is not an easy job and staircase supports about 18 inches long can be bought for 75¢ at most hobby shops and at any dollhouse equipment store. For this house, buy a side-turn staircase for the center location. Balsa wood can be used for the steps. Naturally, the staircase should be painted or stained *before* putting it in the house. Many people who build a dollhouse to display a collection of miniatures prefer not to have a staircase, but if the house is being built to play with, children love to walk their doll families up and down the stairs. Although lightweight dollhouses made with ³/₁₆-inch plywood may be glued together for the most part with epoxy or contact cement, the ³/₈-inch plywood should be nailed. This makes a veritably indestructible house.

FINISHING THE EXTERIOR

The next step is to take the 30-inch strip of wood, which has already been painted, and place this at an angle even with the house and nail at each end. Next nail on the front half of the roof, then attach loose pin hinges to the back side of the strip and attach the back part of the roof to the hinges. If the house is to be used by a small child, loose pin hinges should *not* be used. The reason for this type of hinge is that the back roof can be removed easily and put aside; however, a small child might swallow the pins, and another method of raising the roof should be used. An ordinary stick about 16 inches long could be used to prop the roof, if a block were nailed to the base of the house and another block to the underside of the roof to keep the stick from slipping and the roof crashing down on the head. Another very simple way of supporting the roof is to use a hook-and-eye latch, attaching one part to the chimney and the other part to the roof. These latches can be bought in any hardware store in any size; they are the type used on screen doors. This method, though, would detract somewhat from the appearance of the house.

If the roof has not already been painted, paint it gray and, while waiting for the paint to dry, the chimney can be built from some scraps of plywood. The chimney is 3¹/₄ inches square; the front piece is 6 inches; the back piece is 3¹/₂ inches. The sides are angled by placing the plywood against the slope of the roof (see Fig. 6-4). Draw a line at the slope and cut accordingly. The bottom edges of the front and back will have to be filed or sanded to fit neatly against the roof. Nail the chimney together and then nail it to the front roof, centering it at the top. After attaching the chimney, cover it with the brick paper; if it is covered before attaching, the nails will show.

Once the roof paint has dried thoroughly, the shingles may be applied. This can be done three different ways. Dollhouse "shingle" paper may be bought, but it does not look real at all. Real wood dollhouse shingles may be bought, stained, and glued to the roof, but they are very expensive and it would cost about $20 to shingle a roof this size. The third way, which involves only the cost of a felt-tip pen, is to draw the shingles freehand, as shown in color Fig. 6. The moldings on the front door are also done with a felt-tip pen.

If the exterior was not painted before assembling the house (with the exception of the windows), this should be done now. Allow the paint to dry overnight. Semigloss enamel takes a longer drying time than latex paint, and for this type of house the flat paint is more appropriate. When the paint is completely dry, the stripping or mullions may be put on the windows with Elmer's glue, and the shutters may be attached the same way. Be very careful not to be heavy-handed with the glue; if it smears, it is hard to remove all traces from the plastic windows.

The front door can be put in at this time, saving the handle for last. Attach the real hinges to the door first; then glue on the strap hinges, which have been painted black and, when these are dry, attach the real hinges to the house. When this is done, glue the handle to the door and the Saltbox is finished and ready for furnishing and landscaping.

CHAPTER 8 *Landscaping*

As when building a real house, probably the greatest pleasure comes when the house itself is finished, pristine in its fresh paint with glistening windows. All these original plans, with the exception of the contemporary house, call for a base extending 6 to 8 inches on the sides and front so that they can be landscaped.

Of course, if there is not room for the base and the landscaping, shrubbery and vines can always be painted on the house itself. Many commercial dollhouses are decorated in this way. However, real shrubbery and vines and plants and paths are more attractive.

This landscaping does not have to be expensive, since it all can be made by you. As with everything else concerned with these dollhouses, anything and everything can be bought and will be beautiful, but the costs are prohibitive for most people.

CRAFTING WITH BREAD DOUGH

The formula for bread-and-glue clay is as follows:

3 slices stale bread (remove crusts and shred)
3 tablespoons Elmer's glue
3 tablespoons glycerin

Mix all the ingredients together until the batter feels like dough; it then may be formed into any shape. When hard, it may be painted any color with acrylic paint and it will not break. Whatever is made from this clay *must* be varnished for preservation.

LANDSCAPING SUPPLIES

To do your own landscaping, you will need the following few supplies, depending on how elaborate your garden is going to be.

Plain kitchen sponges, 1" or 2" thick,

Bread dough enough to cut in any shape that is desired

Round toothpicks or very small cardboard lollipop sticks

Sand or *very fine* gravel sold for the bottom of fish tanks

Elmer's glue or DuPont airplane model glue

Paper grass that is sold by the roll in most hobby shops to go with train sets
 or Life-Like grass or dirt which is sprinkled on glue; other landscaping
 products made by Life-Like include trees and stones

Artificial plants with very small leaves, or feathery leaves to make ferns or
 small plants

Florist's wire

Florist's clay

Thimbles for flower pots

MAKING TREES AND SHRUBBERY

To make simple shrubbery around the sides and front of a house, just take
a large sponge and tear it into appropriate shapes, then paint in varying shades
of green and glue to the base or side of the house. For larger-leaved plants, such
as rhododendron, use bought artificial greens such as boxwood: Cut them apart
and regroup the leaves on florist's wire.

The flowers and greenery in the vase shown in Fig. 8-1 are homemade.
The flowers are made from the bread clay and placed on florist's wire for stems.
The greens are a real plant called an *air plant*, which can be bought in any
dime store or florist shop for about 25¢. This plant needs no water and lasts for
months.

To make a topiary tree, take a sponge and cut out two round balls, one
slightly larger than the other (Fig. 8-2). Paint the balls green and, if fruit or
flowers are desired on the trees, these may be made from the bread clay,
painted, then glued on the tree. A lollipop stick or toothpick (depending on the
size of the topiary) can be used as the trunk.

Often, these fruits and flowers will not have to be made from the clay. A
survey of a box or drawer of costume jewelry nearly always will produce a
broken strand of beads that will be just the correct size for small fruits. One
might even be lucky enough to have one earring made of small porcelain
flowers. These can be taken apart and used.

Aside from landscaping, the uses of costume jewelry in dollhouses almost
could be a chapter by itself. A door knocker was made from the gold clip on the
back of an earring. A paperweight for a desk can be made from a large colored
rhinestone from a wornout pin. Even drapery tiebacks can be made by stringing
very small beads or pearls on a wire. Decorative upholstery tacks make excellent
tiebacks.

Fig. 8–1　Bread dough flowers and real air plants

The stone used as a piece of modern sculpture in the atrium of the contemporary house is a piece of polished agate (Fig. 8-2). Beads always can be bunched together on vines or shrubbery to make exotic fruits and flowers. These may be painted or not.

To espalier a tree or make a vine, this can be done with artificial greens and florist's wire (Fig. 8-3). Any other plants or vines, such as those in the atrium, may be made in this same way.

FASHIONING PATHS, PONDS, AND FENCES

Paths may be made by just painting the path area white or gray. For more realism, the path may be drawn on the base, Elmer's glue spread on the path, and sand sprinkled over the glue. The brick path in front of the plantation house was made from dollhouse "brick" paper, which is made to the proper 1:12 scale.

There is indoor landscaping in the Spanish house. The fountain in the hallway was made from bread dough, used for the base, and from a lid of a plastic teapot from a toy tea set (Fig. 8-4). The plants around the base were made from artificial greens set either in thimble or bread dough pots.

If a small pond is desired, either inside or outside the house, the old-fashioned pocketbook mirrors are perfect for this, since they have no frames.

Fig. 8–2 Topiary tree and assorted vines used in atrium of contemporary house

This type of mirror is hard to find nowadays, but similar ones with very narrow frames can be bought in the dime store for just about a dime. The narrow frame can be either painted to blend with the surrounding ground or painted white and, when dry, covered with contact cement and rocks glued all around it.

Fig. 8–3   Spanish hacienda with vines added

Fig. 8-4   Fountain made of bread dough and plastic teapot lid

As shown in the color section, landscaping a dollhouse makes a dramatic improvement and, as with the interior, there really is no end to it. Improvements and changes will always be made, especially as one grows more skillful with practice.

Another real advantage in landscaping your house is that it can hide a multitude of sins that were committed during the construction of the house—a spot where a window was not cut as straight as it might have been or where seams still show from stuccoing the exterior of the Spanish house.

If you prefer to buy the shrubbery instead of making it, there is one good source that is not horribly expensive and will go a long way. This is a box of Lionel bushes and a box of trees. The bushes will cost about $3 and the trees about $4. However, one box of each will be a gracious plenty to do one house. The trees are too small to be used as trees and must be used as bushes. The trunks can be cut off and there are many varieties, including fruit trees. They can be bought both in summer and autumn colors. Hobby shops carry a wide variety of landscaping for model railroad layouts.

If you would like a fence in front of the house, this can be made easily from Popsicle sticks, which can be bought in any chain grocery store, or it may be made from small dowels. Very attractive white plastic fencing is made by Lionel and is not only the correct scale, but is not expensive (Fig. 8-5).

Wrought-iron fencing and gates can be ordered from dollhouse catalogues or shops, but these *are* expensive. If gateposts and finials or some other decorative touch on top is desired, this may be made either from plaster of paris or

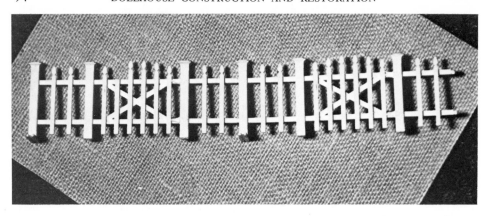

Fig. 8–5   Lionel fencing

bread dough, or simply carved pieces of balsa wood which have been painted or stuccoed.

The ideas for landscaping are endless. Even real plants which have been dried may be used. Of course, after a while these will have to be replaced because even dried plants do not last forever.

If a vacation at the seashore is in store for you, keep the landscaping of the dollhouse in mind and, as you comb the beaches, instead of searching for the largest shells, begin searching for the smallest, including the shell cases which contain myriads of the tiniest shells of all. These shells can be used indoors as well as out. The dollhouse shown in Fig. 9-14 has an aquarium, and in the bottom are real miniature conches from a seed case found on the beach. These perfect conch shells are less than $1/4$ inch long and $1/8$ inch wide. Other shells which are not quite so small may be used around the edge of a pond.

Even with landscaping, the dollhouse person becomes a real scavenger. The world is seen through different eyes; scraps and discards that before were considered useless now have possibilities. Start saving Popsicle sticks and Styrofoam packages that used to be thrown away. These might come in handy.

CHAPTER 9 *Restoration of Old Dollhouses*

A few people are fortunate enough to own an antique dollhouse. Most of the old houses shown in this chapter range from about 1875 to the early 1900s, though there are two from the 1950s and one which dates from the 1930s.

Most antique dollhouses, just as modern ones, were built by loving fathers and grandfathers to house doll families. Very few of these houses were built to scale. This lack of attention to scale did not bother the ten-year-old child in 1875 any more than it would concern the child of today or the adult collector who is fortunate enough to own one. The attention to detail, the sturdiness of construction and the charm of these houses more than makes up for the lack of 1:12 scale prevalent today.

No two old houses will be in identical condition, so the details of renovation will vary. There are a few guiding principles, however. One way to determine the age of your newly acquired dollhouse is to examine the condition of the wood itself. Old ones will be made of real wood, not plywood; older houses will have real hardwood trim, rather than balsa or pine moldings. Commercial dollhouses have always been built to scale (not necessarily 1:12, but with all parts proportionate). Handmade houses have seldom been built to scale.

If your dollhouse has been altered from its original condition, it may be necessary to make a visit to the library to look up architectural and interior details before you can begin the restoration process. You then proceed in much the same way you would set about renovating a real home. Your first step is to scrub it thoroughly inside and out with a mild dishwashing detergent and sponge. You'll have a pretty accurate idea of what needs to be removed, replaced, repaired, painted, stained, sanded, or refinished by the time you have scrubbed every nook and cranny.

Frame repair is the first priority. Some wooden parts may have to be replaced, but it is unlikely that you'll have to resort to this. Do *not* disassemble an old dollhouse entirely, for the wood will probably split when you take it apart or when you attempt to reconstruct it. Gouges or holes in exterior or interior walls or loose joints can be filled with ordinary wood filler or household spackle, then sanded smooth before repainting. If you have to patch a part that will simply be stained later and you can identify the wood, buy wood putty at your local hardware store. You can purchase it in small quantities to match every imagin-

96 DOLLHOUSE CONSTRUCTION AND RESTORATION

able type of wood and, when sanded, it will blend with the wood and can be stained or waxed. If seams and joints of the dollhouse are loose, use contact cement to secure them; hammering on an old house may cause more problems than it cures.

A good soaking with a sponge and hot water will enable you to scrape off wallpaper, but be sure it is beyond repair before you decide to remove it. Wallpapers will be one of the most difficult things to replace if you're trying to match the original; but if you look long enough among dollhouse supplies and gift-wrapping papers, you'll eventually find a substitute that comes close.

If woodwork has been painted repeatedly, you should use a good stripping agent, such as ZAR, and a small putty knife to strip off the old paint before redoing it. Wooden floors can be refinished by sanding lightly, cleaning thoroughly and restaining them or simply waxing them to a shine.

Restoring or replacing interior details, such as lighting fixtures and draperies, will be somewhat difficult if the originals are not intact and salvageable. However, it can be done: Helen Ruthberg's *The Book of Miniatures: Furniture and Accessories*, also published by Chilton, contains detailed instructions for making replicas of interior fixtures and furnishings from every period. You

Fig. 9–1   Restored Edwardian dollhouse, an antique originally made by F.A.O. Schwartz
(*Photo by Mrs. Theodore Condemon*)

could even create wallpaper to match the original, using a scrap that you removed as a pattern. Everything from antique clocks and picture frames to an Early American settee, a Victorian sofa, or a tester bed and cradle can be crafted for your restored treasure or one of the brand new dollhouses in this book.

EDWARDIAN MANSION

There were a number of Edwardian dollhouses, made by the famous New York toy company F.A.O. Schwartz about 1910, that were perfectly to scale. One of these Schwartz dollhouses is shown in Fig. 9-1 and in color Figs. 7 and 12. Originally, this house was a gift for a child. In recent years, it has been beautifully restored by the adult granddaughter and is furnished with many of the original pieces, including the famous F.A.O. Schwartz bathroom of that era with the footed bathtub and the water closet with a chain pull.

The exterior of the Edwardian house needed no repair. The interior was redecorated professionally. The big difference between having a dollhouse restored professionally and doing it yourself is the cost. The wallpapers and matching fabrics used to redecorate are all to scale (1:12) and came from commercial dollhouse suppliers.

GERMANTOWN TOWNHOUSE

The dollhouse shown in Fig. 9-2 and in color Fig. 8 is about 90 years old. It is an exact replica of a real house in the Germantown section of Philadelphia. Although the exterior seems to be built to scale, it is obvious that the interior is not. Interior doors are only 4 inches high, and one of the front rooms is almost completely inaccessible, but it makes no difference. The house is a treasure with its brass widow's walk around the top of the roof, the carved doors, and the real screens in the basement windows below the brass front balconies.

Only one change was made in the restoration of the exterior of this Germantown house. Originally, the widow's walk and balconies were painted dark green. After discovering the solid brass underneath the green paint, it was impossible to resist the temptation not to "do" the exterior exactly as it had been originally (Fig. 9-3). The paint was removed with Strip-Eze, and it was extremely difficult to remove the paint between the tiny ballustrades. An ordinary putty knife or paint scraper is much too big for this kind of work, so a small nail file was used on the base between the brass posts; very fine steel wool was used to remove the layers of paint from the brass. Of course, rubber gloves are a necessity for this type work.

There were not many major repairs that had to be made on this house, as it had been built from heavy lumber. Many of the moldings on both roof and windows had to be replaced (Fig. 9-4) and the front steps were replaced.

Fig. 9–2   Replica of a house in the Germantown section of Philadelphia

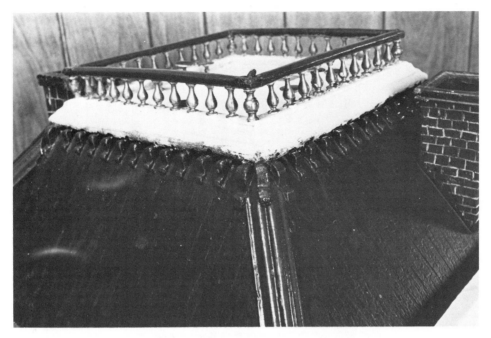

Fig. 9-3   Removing paint to expose genuine brass widow's walk

When replacing the window trim, one trim of each type was removed from a window and used as a pattern. The trims needed were then carved from balsa wood, using an X-acto knife to avoid splitting the wood. They were then painted *before* attaching to the house, which was not done until after the exterior of the house was painted.

The moldings for window trim and the underside of the roof were cut from the same strip of ³/₄-inch-wide molding, 3 feet long (Fig. 9-4). The cost was 25¢. These same strips can be bought in 8-foot pieces at a lumberyard for $1.25. Both the roof and window moldings were copied from the original and painted before being glued on with contact cement. The reason that the molding used on this house was so inexpensive is that it was made from scraps, rather than buying an entire strip.

Since the original windows were of very thin real glass and most were missing, these were replaced with Plexiglas of the same thickness as the original and it was cut professionally for a total cost of $5.

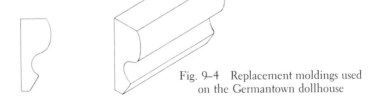

Fig. 9-4   Replacement moldings used on the Germantown dollhouse

Because of the type of construction, the interior first-floor front rooms were difficult to restore or refinish. The back rooms were simple, since the whole back of the house opens; the second floor was easy because the roof lifts off. It was impossible to salvage the gold moiré living room wallpaper, so a new paper with a Victorian motif was chosen. With the open back and solid construction, this is a dollhouse that is just as suitable for a child as for a serious collector of miniatures.

GERMAN MANSION

The third dollhouse was bought in Germany about 1880 or 1890 (Figs. 9-5 and 9-6). This house is now being enjoyed by three generations. It has never been restored and still holds the original furnishings. Note the painted swags on the front. This house is built on the same principle as the 1890 Schwartz dollhouse, that is, in having the front open up for play instead of the back (Fig. 9-5). The roof also lifts off in order to be able to reach the third floor. One par-

Fig. 9-5   Interior of German house, with the front open

Fig. 9–6   German dollhouse, c. 1880

ticularly interesting feature of the German house is that, since it contains the original furnishings, as it has been enjoyed by later generations, the furnishings of those eras also have been added, which makes it seem more of a real house than a play house.

VICTORIAN HOUSE

Dollhouse number four is an elaborate Victorian design of the type found in many small towns during the late 1800s and early 1900s (color Fig. 9). This one is very narrow and very tall. It is only 21 inches wide and 18 inches deep. As can be seen in Figure 9-7, the sides of this house open instead of the front or back. Painting and interior decoration were all the restoration necessary for this house. Some outside moldings were replaced and the house was wired for electrical lighting.

STUCCO FARMHOUSE

Dollhouse number five is a simple stucco farmhouse of the late 1800s. This house is 23 inches wide and only 15 inches deep. It has not been restored. The steep peaked gable in the front gives the house more interest, and this is one of the few houses of that age that has an open back (Fig. 9-8 and color section, Fig. 13).

TURN-OF-THE-CENTURY DOLLHOUSE

Dollhouse number six, which dates from 1900, has a painted gray "stone" exterior (Fig. 9-9). The roof base of wood tile seems to be of papier mâché or some kind of heavy cardboard available during the early part of this century. None of the rooms go all the way through. Both the front and back of this house open which, of course, is typical for a house of this age. The wallpaper is original and is interesting with its trompe-l'oeil effect of seeing into further rooms.

The size is standard for its age. It is 16 inches wide with two rooms per floor; it is 18 inches deep and 25 inches high at the tip of the roof. The entire roof lifts off, as with the Germantown and German houses but, unlike those, a ceiling has been nailed across the top of the second floor, and the second floor rooms cannot be reached from above.

Fig. 9–7   Victorian dollhouse—the sides open instead of the back

Fig. 9–8   Stucco farmhouse, c. 1890

Fig. 9–9   Gray stone dollhouse from the turn of the century

BARBIE DOLL HOUSE

This house was built by a father for his daughter's Barbie Doll about 20 years ago. It is constructed of $1/4$-inch plywood and is 22 inches wide, with three stories and three rooms (Fig. 9-10). It has shutters and windowboxes, which

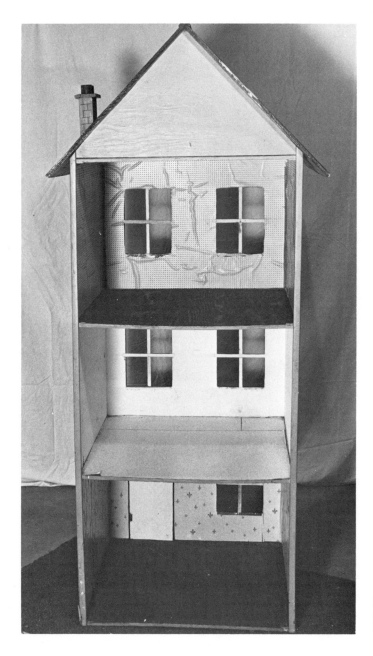

Fig. 9–10 Interior of three-room Barbie Doll house

required some work to restore (Fig. 9-11). The chimney is a block of wood with two pieces of doweling added for chimney pots. It has no windows, just the panes.

The interior still has to be redone. The Contact paper will be removed, new wallpaper hung, and the floors refinished.

Fig. 9-11 Exterior of house for Barbie Doll; note windowboxes and chimney construction

REMODELING A VARIETY OF ARCHITECTURAL STYLES

The Main Street bungalow in Fig. 9-12 dates from the 1930s. It is 24 inches long and 14^1/$_2$ inches high. The ceilings are only 6 inches high, which is unusual because this appears to be a commercial dollhouse with only four rooms.

Circa 1956, the dollhouse in Fig. 9-13 was not commercially built and is quite large. It is 36 inches wide, 18^1/$_2$ inches deep, and 28 inches high. The windows are of real glass and the chimney, which is a solid piece of wood, is covered with patterned Contact paper rather than being painted.

Dollhouse number nine is not old and started as a kit. The kit was designed by Craft House, but the builder has added windows at the sides, as well as a greenhouse. She has gone into great detail on the interior, installing bookcases, cabinets, and a tile fireplace, so that this hardly qualifies as a "kit" dollhouse any longer (Fig. 9-14).

The knobs on the cabinets are the heads of tailor's or dressmaker's pins. The tiles around the fireplace are made from embossed wallpaper which was painted with small scenes on each square, then coated with Mod-Podge, a decoupage product. Two or three coats will give a "china" or "tile" effect.

Fig. 9–12   Commercially made 1930s dollhouse with only four rooms

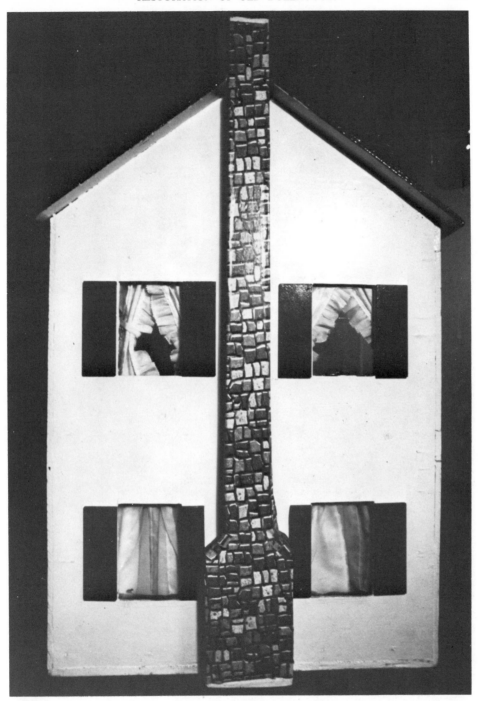

Fig. 9–13   An unusual chimney was found on this house, c. 1956

Fig. 9–14   Interior details of this house were all handmade

Fig. 9–15   Exterior of A-frame contemporary house

The A-frame house shown in Figs. 9-15 and 9-16 and color Fig. 10 was made by John Rembold of Mt. Lake Park, Maryland. Although the house is not to scale, it has an interesting design and is sturdy enough for any child to enjoy. This one is quite large. It is 33 inches wide and 33 inches high at the roof. The shutters and windowbox were added by the author.

Fig. 9–16   Interior of the A-frame

CHAPTER 10 *Bookshelf Dollhouses*

The dollhouse shown in Fig. 10-1 is a so-called bookshelf dollhouse for obvious reasons. This type, of course, really is not a house at all. It is a display case for miniature furniture. The bookshelf house is perfect for collectors who want to exhibit their furniture. Bookshelf houses have been in use in this country for over a hundred years. They were popular during the early 1800s, and many are found in museums. This type also can be fun for a child who

Fig. 10–1   Bookshelf dollhouse for displaying miniature collections

112

lives in a small apartment and might not have the space for a full-sized doll-house.

BUILDING A DISPLAY CASE

The construction of such a shelf is certainly very simple. For a four-room house of plywood, it should be 24 inches long, 10 inches deep, and 18 inches high (Fig. 10-2). The 18-inch height will provide ceilings approximately 9 inches high—slightly less, to allow for the ³/₈-inch thickness of the plywood. There will be four rooms, 10 by 12 inches. Other types of wood may be used, and the back may be either plywood or Masonite. One advantage of this type of house is that rooms can be added at any time.

Since this is not meant to be a replica of a real house, there are no doors or windows. Windows can be painted on the inside if curtains are desired to give a more realistic effect.

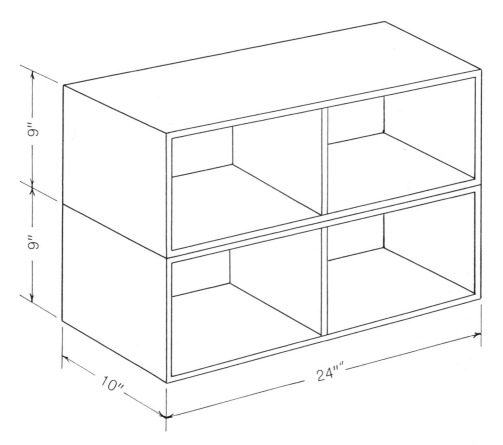

Fig. 10–2   Building a bookshelf case from plywood

A bookshelf house can be made even from a wooden fruit box, especially the type that has a divider in the middle. Since fruit boxes are made from such rough wood, a good deal of sanding would be necessary before doing any papering or painting.

Just because these are not houses on the exterior does not mean that they cannot be finished as elaborately as one desires on the interior.

A staircase could be installed, using the commercial supports available, or making your own (see Fig. 4-10). There are beautiful staircases of many designs that are made commercially. These are complete and many have landings. They are very expensive, starting in price at about $8 or $9. These are ready for staining or painting.

The bookshelf house can be wired for electricity. There are dozens of miniature light fixtures available. The builder may prefer to have a spotlight on the shelves instead. In doing this he is not limited in choice just to the commercial fixtures and can design his own of silver, gold, or crystal (tin, brass, or glass).

If one has an interest in the decorative arts of a particular period or country, whether it is seventeenth-century France or twentieth-century America, the bookshelf house is ideal for this kind of collection. The collector may start with one room at a time and add another as each one is completed to his liking. Usually, once a collector starts with his bookshelf rooms, he never finishes. The project can last for a lifetime because there is always room for improvement.

Bookshelf or showcase dollhouses are not exclusively for the use of little girls and adults. A young boy might enjoy having his own auto garage and repair shop. The showcase could be transformed into the interior of an airline terminal, a police station, or a firehouse. The possibilities are endless and

Fig. 10–3   Furnished dining room in display case

require little money, little space, and endless imagination. An example follows of a simple showcase house with a realistic exterior.

CONSTRUCTING A SHOWCASE DOLLHOUSE

The dollhouse shown in Fig. 10-4 and in the color section, Fig. 11, was built from plans offered by *McCall's Needlework and Crafts* magazine. Richard Pyle, M.D., of Albuquerque, New Mexico, built it for his daughter, Chris.

An interesting feature of this house is that it is the side that is open. The house is $18^1/_2$ inches across the open side and 26 inches high at the peak of the roof.

Dr. Pyle decided to leave the top floor open to give an extra usable room. Rather than enclosing it with a triangular piece as called for in the plans, he fashioned roof supports from $^3/_4$-inch stock.

The roofing material is basswood lapped siding, scored vertically with an awl and bradded to the exterior walls. The fireplace is built of pine stock, painted black inside, scored outside, and painted red. There is a tiny oven next to the fireplace; the door works and is hinged with model airplane flap hinges. All parts of the house were painted with white enamel or finished with urethane varnish before assembly.

The influence of the Southwest can be seen in young Chris Pyle's house. In Fig. 10-5 and in color Fig. 11, you can just see the little Acoma Pueblo adobe bread oven in the grass and the tiny silver bowl created by a Pueblo silversmith, near the front door. Chris has furnished the dollhouse with a miniature Navajo rug and tiny baskets from Juarez, Mexico, to house her German doll, a gift from her father.

Fig. 10–4   Showcase dollhouse

Fig. 10–5   Interior furnishings reflect Southwest influence

Sources of Supply

There are dozens of catalogues available, selling every conceivable type of dollhouse equipment. Many of the same products will be seen in most of the catalogues; however, it is a good idea to order several when you plan to build or restore, in order to have a thorough knowledge of what is available and the cost. In some instances, a catalogue will show a living-room sofa for $14 and have a kit available so you can build the identical sofa for $4. The kits can be easily assembled by following detailed instructions. They are the same type kits as those for model ships or planes.

Abigail's
Box 28
Mapleville, RI 02839

Wallpaper (send 25¢ for samples, refundable with order)

Betty's Doll House
Cates Plaza, Suite 117
375 Pharr Road, NW
Atlanta, GA 30305

Old dollhouses; variety of furnishings

H. L. Childs & Son, Miniatures
25 State St.
Northhampton, MA 01060

Hardware; building materials, such as staircases, doors, bay windows; furnishings and accessories

Chestnut Hill Studio
Box 907
Taylors, SC 29687

Fine period furniture, building materials, sterling silver (send $3 for catalogue)

Craft-Creative Kit
Dept. 70, North Ave., Rt. 83
Elmhurst, IL 60126

Light fixtures (send $1 for catalogue)

Downs
Dept. 2212-A
Evanston, IL 60204

Furnishings and accessories (send 25¢ for catalogue)

Enchanted Toy Shop
23812 Lorain Rd.
North Olmsted, OH 44070

Furnishings; building materials (separate catalogues, send 50¢ each)

Green Door Studio 517 E. Annapolis St. St. Paul, MN 55118	Wallpaper, floor coverings, accessories, furniture patterns (send 50¢ for catalogue)
Leisure Time Publications 111 Sandstone Drive Rochester, NY 14616	Furnishings and accessories
Miles Kimball Oshkosh, WI 54901	Furnishings and accessories; some lighting fixtures
Mini Mundus 1030 Lexington Ave. New York, NY 10021	Furnishings and accessories (catalogue, $2)
The Mystic River Guild 13 Water St. Mystic, CT 06355	Accessories
New Hampton General Store RFD Hampton, NJ 08827	Furnishings and accessories
S. W. Randall Toys & Gifts 5856 Forbes Ave. Pittsburgh, PA 15217	Fine period furniture and accessories (catalogue, 25¢)
School House Miniatures P.O. Box 432 Pawleys Island, SC 29585	Furnishings and accessories
B. Shackman & Co. 85 Fifth Ave. New York, NY 10003	Furnishings and accessories
The Stitchery Dept. 113, 204 Worcester Turnpike Wellesley, MA 02181	Dollhouse needlepoint
Taggart's Toys and Hobbies 11 N. Franklin Chagrin Falls, OH 44024	Building materials; lighting fixtures; wallpapers
Windfall 62 Windfall Bldg. Sharon Springs, NY 13459	Furnishings and accessories (catalogue, 25¢)

Index

Page numbers in **bold** type indicate information in illustrations

Nina Joyner has been constructing and renovating dollhouses as a hobby for a number of years. Her interest in this subject started in a related field. She developed a skill for furniture refinishing out of necessity in the early days of her marriage.

She is the author of *Furniture Refinishing at Home*, published by Chilton. She has made a number of television appearances, lectured at clubs, and has done feature writing for the *Main Line Chronicle* in Ardmore, Pennsylvania. Nina Joyner was listed in *Who's Who of American Women*.

Having moved from the Philadelphia area in 1972, she now lives in Pittsburgh with her husband, a cardiologist, and their two children.